3/91

THEBES

Giorgio A. Livraga

THEBES

Translated from the Spanish by Julian Scott

NEW ACROPOLIS, Publishers
Humanistic, Philosophical and Esoteric Sciences
Valencia, Spain

Copy right by NUEVA ACROPOLIS
First published 1986
by NUEVA ACROPOLIS
Catalans, 6 - Valencia
English translation published 1989
by NUEVA ACROPOLIS
Printed and bound in Turkey
ISBN 975-7502-00-6

This handbook is dedicated to all my disciples who are eager to make contact with that Mystery which we call Egypt, through one of its countless and most beautiful expressions. And to the Genius of memory which causes me once more to whisper the litany which is set down in the Book of the Hidden Dwelling:

"BLESSED IS HE WHO LIVES, BLESSED HE WHO DIES IN THEBES

CONTENTS

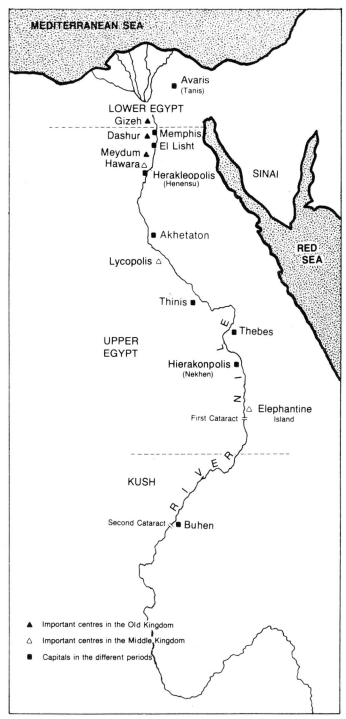

Map of Egypt showing the main political centres in antiquity

INTRODUCTION

Any subject concerning the human past should be approached with the utmost caution; for just as there is a veil which prevents us from seeing into the future although there may be signs that portend it, and though logic may enable us to deduce the outcome of events, there is another which stands between us and the forms of the past and renders them blurred and incomprehensible .

Anyone who believes that the historical and archaeological sciences in general are exact, knows little of the cyclic and evolutionary process of these disciplines themselves and the fascinating yet laborious task of continual interpretation of the ever-changing conceptions, to which the investigator, inevitably pressurized by his own bias and that of his age, is subject.

The ancient Greeks gave the name *Egypt* to the ancient Land of Kem, which means mystery and enigma.

And within that enigma we have chosen the area of the ancient city which the Greeks, again, called *Thebes of the*

Hundred Gates, to distinguish it from the other Greek city, which they referred to as *Thebes of the Seven Gates.*

This in itself is a mystery. For it is inconceivable that the Egyptians, from what we know of their works, would have been so architecturally unintelligent as to build the gates side by side. And if we take into account that the man of pre-industrial times would think nothing of walking several kilometres to get from one place to another, the gates must have been at least 500 metres apart. This would give the city (multiplying 500 by 100) a perimeter of 50,000 metres, which is completely at variance with the findings of modern archaeology and aerial observation. The city which was figuratively referred to by both Egyptians and Greeks, that mysterious city which was the centre of the priestly government of Amon, did not cover such an enormous area. And of its walls only insignificant remains still stand.

Did the Greeks, then, say a hundred as a synonym of "many"?... This is something that perhaps we shall never know.

Some contemporary authors have conceived the idea that enormous area also included the western bank of the Nile, *the City of the Dead.* But the particular natura of the Valley which lies in the shadow of the Western Mountain, and the total absence of any traces of walls, prevents us from giving reasonable credence to these hypotheses which the sense of desperation in the face of the incomprehensible is in the habit of bringing forth.

Nevertheless, if we are to walk across the burning sands of Egypt, traversed by the only great river in the world which flows from South to North, we must learn to become accustomed to the incomprehensible, the enigmatic, the mysterious and the hieratic... yet profoundly human.

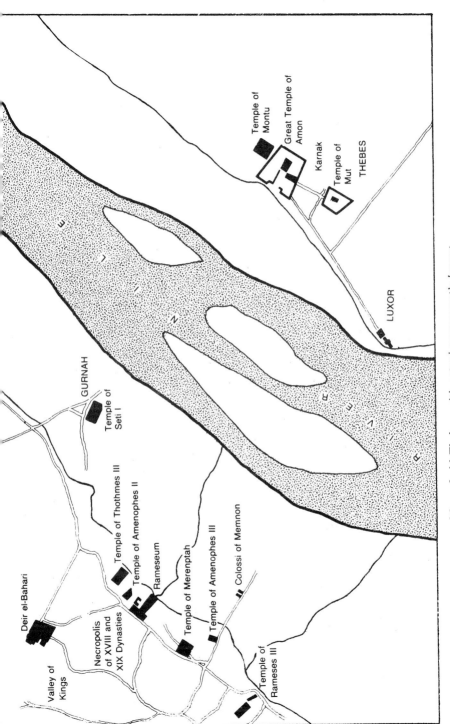

Map of old Thebes, with actual monument's layout

CHRONOLOGY

"Thebes existed before any other place; water and earth were there at the beginning of time, and the creation of the World and the Gods took place in Thebes, by the grace of its God, Amon."

(Papyrus from the time of Rameses II)

Every nation, whether Hebrew, Chinese, Maya or Greek, has always regarded itself as the most ancient on Earth, and in this the Egyptians were no exception. But behind the masks of geopolitics and time these traditions all ultimately refer to a Heavenly Man, the Archetype of all Humanity, and the city - in this case Thebes - is the material birthplace of that Man, as in the Hindu myth of Agni, in the Rig Veda, who is born in a stable of wood and straw which catch fire on contact with him.

Such accounts are summarily categorized under the broad heading of "Mythologies" - except by their believers,

for whom they are Sacred History, as in the case of the Bible for the Hebrews and Christians - and are regarded by scientists as being at best merely allegorical and without historical foundation.

But the realization of one's ignorance is a first step in the direction of knowledge even if it is not knowledge itself, and this has led to other more reliable sources of information being sought. Contrary to popular belief, however, it is very difficult to date something exactly, since the stratigraphical methods are frequently inapplicable, and the modern equipment for measuring radioactivity and the variations in natural magnetization are only able to operate with precision in exceptional cases. And when it comes to stones and other inorganic materials, dating is done by comparison. But if these current methods of research were still in existence in a thousand years' time, and an attempt were made to date the Sphinx of Gizeh by reference to a fire which had been lit at its feet in the last few years, it would be considered to be contemporary with the supersonic aircraft Concorde.

Egyptologists today are still working on the basis, with few variations, of a chronology which was put forward by an Egyptian priest of indeterminate existence, whom the Classical Greeks named Manetho. This man divided the History of Egypt according to Dynasties or changes of family in the rulers, within the context of a continuous Theocracy believed to have sprung from the Regent Gods of the Country of Kem themselves. Thus, the King or Pharaoh was the embodiment of a Cosmic Order, and his figure is rendered impersonal by a more or less uninterrupted succession, although we know today that there were Dynasties like the XVth, which were really no more than ephemeral transitions, and that what Manetho calls "years" do not necessarily correspond to periods of 365 days, since in Ancient Egypt there were at least three interlocking calendar systems.

An example of a Chronological Table is the one presented by Michalowsky and his adherents, of which the following is a summary:

PREHISTORY
Before 4000BC. Stone Age period.

Settlements at El-Fayun, Merindeh-Beni, Salameh and El-Omari, in Lower Egypt; Tasi and Badari in Upper Egypt.

From 4000BC to 3000BC. Chalcolithic, Eneolithic or Predynastic period.

In the South, connected with the Culture of Badaria and Nagada; in the North, with the so-Called Heliopolis Culture.

ARCHAIC PERIOD
From 3100BC to 2686BC. Dynasty I and Dynasty II.

The first Dynasty is dominated by the figure of Menes, a great king according to reports gathered from the faithful by Herodotus, who, amongst other prodigious exploits, founded the city of Memphis. Menes is also called Narmer and to him is attributed the famous stone palette, which was probably used for ceremonial purposes. It is called the Thinite Period, after the city of Thinis, which has never been found.

Cartouche of the Pharaoh Menes

The second is the period during which Memphis is thought to have developed and the first step pyramids, or system of tombs covered with tumuli, to have been built. Other authors believe that this did not occur until the following period.

OLD KİNGDOM
From 2686BC to 2181BC. Covers the period from the third Dynasty to the sixth.

According to some authors, this was the real Memphite Era which saw the building of Zoser's pyramid at Saqqara and the great works of the White City complex (during the 3rd Dynasty), masterminded by the architect, doctor and magician Imhotep, who was later to be deified and associated with Aesculapius and Seraphis.

Zoser's pyramid at Saqqara

The 4th Dynasty led into the reigns of Snefru, Kheops, Khephren and Mykerinos, as he was called by the Greeks. These are generally credited with the building of the three pyramids which bear their names today, although the attribution is very doubtful.

Cartouche of the Pharaoh Kheops

The 5th Dynasty is comprised of Sahu-re, Ni-weser-re and Unas. The latter is credited with the construction of the pyramid - today externally in ruins - which contains the ancient ritual known as the Pyramid Texts, which have only been partially translated, and from which the Greeks are said to have taken the famous book of aphorisms and maxims, only partly preserved, called *the Kybalion.*

Cartouche of the Pharaoh Sahu-re

Cartouche of the Pharaoh Unas

The 6th Dynasty is occupied by Tety and Pepy. It is regarded as an epoch of great cultural and political expansion.

FIRST INTERMEDIATE PERIOD
From 2181BC to 2133BC. Extends from the 7th to the 10th Dynasty.

This is marked by the occurrence of great revolutions, maritime invasions and cataclysms. Egypt lapses into a kind of feudal period or Middle Ages. The first

two Dynasties continue at Memphis and the 9th and 10th are governed from a city which the Greeks called Herakleopolis.

MIDDLE KINGDOM
From 2133BC to 1786BC. Spans the 11th and 12th Dynasties.

The first is that of the Mentuhoteps and the second of the Amonemhats and the Senuserts. The old sanctuary of Thebes emerges as the capital of the Empire. Memphis is said to be in ruins. Ceramics and metallurgy flourish. Industry appears to develop, but the outstanding works of architecture, like the Great Pyramid, are not to be repeated. In the papyri and engravings frequent allusions are made to a past splendour which may perhaps be that of the First Dynasties or maybe of others which are not mentioned here.

SECOND INTERMEDIATE PERIOD
From 1786BC to 1650BC. Extends from the 13th Dynasty to the 16th.

We have few details about this confused period. The 13th Dynasty is ruled by the Sebekhoteps and the Neferhoteps. The 14th by the Unknown Kings. And in the 15th and 16th comes the great invasion of the Hyksos or "commoners", who are assimilated into the Egyptian culture, as we can see from the thousands of geometrically patterned scarabs in ceramic and stone that were manufactured during this period. It is still not clear why they left Egypt, and some fragments of papyri state that they were so repugnant that after their departure the palace flagstones over which they had passed were taken up.

NEW KINGDOM
From 1650 BC to 1085BC. Extends from the 17th to the 20th Dynasty.

The 17th is based at Thebes, with Kames. The 18th includes several very important figures. Its Pharaohs are Aahmes, the Amonhoteps, the Thothmes, Hatshepsut, Akhenaten, Tutankhamon and Haremheb.

Aahmes dealt the final blow to the Hyksos invasions and Amonhotep I created the New Kingdom, the most well known of the three. Thothmes I and Thothmes II reconquered all the territory which had been lost and added new lands to the Empire of the Double Crown. Hatshepsut ruled in the name of his legitimate successor Thothmes III and went to the extent of presenting herself in the guise of a man. She had a fruitful reign and sent naval expeditions to the land of Punt, a subject of controversy among specialists, the current belief being that she sailed around the whole of Africa with her great fleet, which gives it more the appearance of a punitive military expedition than of a trade mission. It is possible that her ships, with their light yet sturdy construction, swept away the pirates who infested the Red Sea and the Arabian Sea. It is said that they left several fortified ports behind them to prevent further invasions, which Egypt had not forgotten. It is the first ocean-going Egyptian fleet that we know of. On their return, they brought back exotic animals and plants, like incense, which were then cultivated in Egypt. The Theban Theocracy accepted her until her death. She was succeeded by the extraordinary Thothmes III, a great Initiate, scholar, conqueror and soldier who made seventeen expeditions into Asia. Amonhotep IV became a great heretic, who left Thebes and had an ephemeral

capital built at Tel-El-Amarna. He fought against the Mysteries, and Egypt was thrown into a war of religions which weakened it and broke down its Asian frontiers. He was a good poet but a dreadful ruler and probably a homosexual. In Egypt more than seventy pyramids had been built, and it is said that this Pharaoh had several of these sacked and destroyed, together with the "cartouches" of their names. (This word, meaning "cartridges", is a modern denomination given to them on account of the oval shape, connected with the Key of Life, in which the names are enclosed.) He reigned for seventeen years and committed suicide or was poisoned by a glass of wine.

Modern theories claim that Smenkhkare was the real companion of this Pharaoh and that the beautiful Nefertiti was only his official wife. His exoteric religion, a cult to the Sun Disk, died with him. Great transformations had taken place in art, which had diverged from the initiatic canons, and the young Tutankhamon was buried in a secondary tomb with several typical and almost unaltered pieces of Tel-El-Amarna art, as can be seen in the articles of gilded furniture. Moreover, the reinstated Initiatic Brotherhood of Amon in Thebes overloaded him with protective treasures and amulets, as Carter was able to reveal to the world, for although his tomb had begun to be looted, it had been rapidly restored to its original condition by the "police" of the Valley of the Kings. Haremheb, the general who is said to have received the sceptre of power from the talons of a golden Hawk, was the one who restored Egypt's frontiers, pacified its inhabitants and enriched them with a new and vigorous organization. Having completed his mission, he received a Pharaoh's honours at his death,

and with him the 18th Dynasty came to an end, since he left no heirs.

The 19th Dynasty inludes Seti I, Rameses II and Menephtah. Seti I rebuilt the upper part of the Initiatic Sanctuary of Abydos, which was popularly held to be the tomb of Osiris; he restored the temple of Karnak and enlarged it, amongst other important architectural works, and still found time to carry out military campaigns to strengthen the frontiers in Syria. Rameses II, who reigned for sixty-seven years and is today believed to have lived for about a hundred, led the second campaign against the Hittites, who were already very powerful, and was renowned for his part in the great chariot battle of Kadesh, with his tamed lions. He was represented at Abu-Simbel and was a great builder praised in all the temples. His principal wife was Nefertari. His successor, Menephtah, kept order in the Empire and expelled several nomadic tribes.

The 20th Dynasty extends from Rameses III to Rameses XI. Apart from Rameses III, a great figure whose exploits in battle are represented in the temple of Medinet, we have little individual information about the other Rameses, although the study of the crypts in the Valley of the Kings reveals an age of splendour which gradually declined, while the priests of the different temples hastened to gather up the old teachings and conceal the kings' mummies in secret secondary burials, since the course of Egypt's destiny was approaching its end.

LATE PERIOD
This extends from the year 1085BC to 332BC and from Dynasty XXI to XXX.

Some authors include here the Third Intermediate Period with the 21st Dynasty at Tanis and other cities in the North and South, when the Empire disintegrated into another feudal era or Middle Ages, followed by a Libyan epoch with the 22nd, 23rd and 24th Dynasties, an Ethiopian with the 25th and then a Saite with the 26th Dynasty. Egypt was in ruins, but there is one fact worth noting in connection with Necho II (a Pharaoh of the 26th Dynasty): the opening of a communication via a system of canals between the Nile Delta and the Red Sea. Part of his work was re-utilized in the 19th century in the building of the Suez Canal.

After a disastrous war with Babylon came the Persian domination, the 27th Dynasty under the harsh tutelage of Cambyses, Darius and Xerxes. Many ancient ceremonies, like that of the Apis Bull, were abolished, and temples and libraries were destroyed. The canals began to silt up. The underwater temples, like that of Abydos, ceased to function. The Initiates were reduced to tiny groups and the correct reading of the hieratic hieroglyphics began to be forgotten. The 28th and 29th Dynasties, known as the Mendesian, were unable to halt the disintegration.

The 30th, of the Nectanebos, took advantage of the magnetic current which shot across Mediterranean Europe with the birth of the exceptional Alexander the Great, who called himself a son of Amon, conceived on Egyptian soil. Before dying in Babylon in 323BC he was crowned King of Egypt in Memphis. But the Dynasties had ended.

◀ Page 22
*Rameses II represented on one
of the colossi of the facade of
the temple of Abu-Simbel in Nubia*

MACEDONIAN EPOCH
From the year 332BC to 304BC.

The city of Alexandria grew larger and larger and a Greek administration replaced the now antiquated Egyptian one.

LAGEID or PTOLEMAIC EPOCH
From 304BC to 30BC.

Egypt experienced a fleeting splendour as a result of a new administration, the growing importance of the now great city of Alexandria and the undoubted genius of the Ptolemies who, with their general love of culture, oversaw the restoration of temples, roads and canals. Alexandria came to be the Mediterranean's largest and most important city. Until its last Queen, Cleopatra, clashed with Rome and - after the murder of her husband Julius Caesar and her last attempt to remarry, with Mark Anthony - was defeated at Actium by Octavius and committed suicide, as tradition has it, by having herself bitten by an asp.

ROMAN PERIOD
From 30BC to 395.

Egypt then became part of the Roman Empire. There were further restorations of temples, some as unfortunate as that of the North Colossus of Memnon, which ceased to emit its mysterious musical note. Bound to the destiny of Rome, Egypt fell with the Empire. It was broken up by thousands of religious and political sects. Bands of barbarians and booty-hunters smashed

and looted everything they could find. Many beautiful paintings were whitewashed with lime. Statues were disfigured and demolished. Alexandria itself suffered the disastrous effects of the appearance of the High Middle Ages. Its philosophers were murdered like Hypatia, or persecuted like Marcion. The famous Library, which had already had an accidental fire in the Roman civil wars, now suffered another at the hands of the Christians.

BYZANTINE PERIOD
From 395 to 641.

The looting and destruction went on. The last Initiates perished at Philae. Those who did not convert to Christianity were stoned or hounded into exile.

ARABIC PERIOD
From 641.

This saw the final burning of the remains of the Library of Alexandria by the Caliph Omar. The converts to Christianity became transformed into the modern Copts, and the majority became Muslims. The Sphinx and the temples were gradually buried by the sand. The cycle of Egyptian Civilization had now finally come to an end.

DOUBTS ABOUT THE OFFICIALLY
ACCEPTED CHRONOLOGY

It is obvious that not everything that official science accepts at one time in history has to be true, and what one century affirms is in many cases denied by the next.

This has been seen as "the great virtue" of the Science which grew up under the wing of Encyclopaedism, in that it is not afraid to contradict itself in its search for the truth. Yet this is only partially true, since, on the one hand, Science, or rather scientists, *are* afraid to contradict themselves; and if they retract any of their former statements, they do so only with the greatest reluctance when the tide of fresh research has overwhelmed them with different data. Moreover, the dogmatic manner of presenting scientific knowledge does nothing to encourage any revision of past research, since it is already accepted as being true. Unfortunately, this is not the case, although the works of popular writers and of many learned academics make it appear so.

When we come to History, that is to the sufficiently well known part of the human past - according to the most common of its definitions - we have very little information even about events as recent as many of those of the Second World War. If to this we add the fact that, as the saying goes, "History is written by the winners", we find ourselves almost without criteria by which to judge the events of the past. This is if we are really seeking the truth and not a substitute for it to fill the emptiness which has been left in our minds by the knowledge that the stories in the Bible are no more than allegories, whether esoteric or just plain misleading, depending on the capacity of interpretation of the person who is analysing them. For there is always the occasional nugget of gold to be found amid so much sand, like the historical references to certain peoples of antiquity, as long as one leaves aside, of course, the eternal commentaries about the wrath of the God of Israel.

What is needed, therefore, is an eclectic spirit - philosophical and scientific in the true sense of this word to enable us to reach valid conclusions. These may not shed great amounts of light, but would at least diminish the darkness which engulfs things, and make it possible for us to see them in their approximate dimensions, even if the details may escape us.

We have seen that, for official science, Egypt passed from a period in which men worked stones in the Neolithic manner, lacked writting and obviously any non-utilitarian notion of art and architecture, surrounded by a fauna which included crudely represented giraffes and elephants, to the erection of monuments whose perfection we are still describing, with geodesic orientations superior to those of the astronomical observations of the 19th century, all in the space of... 900 years!

In other words, a period of time equivalent to that which separates the iron fish-hook from the steel fish-hook, the Gothic cathedral from the modern church... Less than 1000 years!

This attracts attention without calling forth any stronger epithet than "remarkable"

Let us make a succinct analysis of the situation.

a) The Capsian epoch, a branch of the Higher Palaeolithic in the area of Egypt, presents extremely poor characteristics in comparison with the Aurignacion and the Magdalenian epochs which are attributed to the same period in Europe. Thus it is illogical that Egypt should have developed such a formidable civilization 3000 years before higher cultures had begun to exist in Europe, which were incapable, moreover, of expressing themselves through constructions like the pyramids of Gizeh.

b) The total incompatibility of the Nagada culture with its apparent logical continuation into the Archaic, properly Egyptian, period.

c) What are called the Thinite Dynasties are, according to current opinion, subsequent to Menes; half a century ago, they were said to be earlier and Menes or Narmer, then known as the Unifier of Egypt, was placed in the 3rd Dynasty. But current discoveries reveal a structure of Nomes or provinces which were already perfectly established in the 1st Dynasty. This would confirm the role attributed to Menes by classical writers as initiator of the "historical Dynasties" of Egypt. But if they were already unified and organized into provinces and had already won several political victories, as testified by the palette of the same King Narmer, how

Palette of Narmer, Cairo's Museum

Gizeh Pyramids

could they have been, a few years earlier, Eneolithic savages far inferior to their contemporaries on the European continent, who had only emerged from the Stone Age - with few exceptions - at the beginning of the first Millennium BC?

Let us remember that in this famous *Gallic Wars* Julius Caesar states - with all the immense authority given him by his intelligence and by the fact that he was an eye witness - that apart from celtic tribes, even in the 1st century BC the other peoples of continental Europe fought crudely, lived in huts, offered human sacrifices (this also applies to the Celts) and had no cities or temples to demonstrate a basic knowledge of stone carving and fitting, and knew nothing about the construction of bridges or of irrigation channels. Where centres of civilization did exist, they were few and far between and always stemmed from colonies which had been settled from the Mediterranean basin. He found nothing even remotely resembling what had already existed thirty centuries earlier in Egypt.

d) Many important monuments, like the Great Pyramid, are undatable. In this particular case, the building, which is totally lacking in inscriptions, was "slotted into" the time of Kheops because of the seal of a cartouche which states his name incorrectly (or that of Kem, by which Egypt was formerly known), on a plaster facing of one of the storage chambers above the so-called King's chamber. To our knowledge, it has apparently hardly occurred to anyone, though the idea is simple, that this seal, besides being rather dubious, might well have been made subsequent to the actual building of the monument, especially in view of the fact that there are frequent cases in Egypt of objects even as small as the tiny funerary statuettes known as *ou-*

31

shabtis being re-utilized. The same has happened with the Sphinx of Gizeh, with the difference that the latter offers absolutely nothing which allows it to be dated, apart from the stone tablet left by Thothmes IV stating that in his epoch, the 18th Dynasty, it was already completely buried by the sand and it was only because of a kind of parapsychological dream that he was led to find it and restore it to view.

Face of the Sphinx of Gizeh and stele of Thothmes IV

The fundamental error is not that official science should offer its opinion on the chronological question, but that it gives it as if it were absolute and unappealable, when it is based on such flimsy, and sometimes practically non-existent, evidence.

e) Many of Egypt's greatest monuments, which were enlarged, improved and restored in different

epochs, simply could not have been built using the methods and materials which are supposed to have been used, at least as far as their main structures are concerned. For example, the great ramp which was supposedly erected perpendicular to one of the sides of the Great Pyramid to support the enormous loads, would have had to have been encased in walls of immense stones, at least 1600 metres in length. There have been no traces or ruins found of any such ramps which, to be functional, would have had to have been at least of comparable size if not larger than the very pyramid that they were helping to build.

In his *Timaeus and Critias*, Plato gives a detailed account, gathered from the Egyptian priests and replete with extremely precise technical data, of the city which crowned the last remaining part of Atlantis. Yet he never said a word about these other technologies, which one would expect him to have been told about in Egypt itself, and which, moreover, do not figure in any reliefs and have left no remains. In spite of everything, the methods used to build the Great Pyramid are constantly reaffirmed. And the same happens with the temple of Karnak and the Osirion of Abydos.

Leaving aside the fantasies about extra-terrestrials, for which there is not the least evidence either, the truth is that we do not know how many of those monuments were built. Nor how they managed to drill with such apparent ease, as measurements of the number of revolutions used in the cutting operations are now showing, through the extremely hard diorite of the Canopic jars, since they had no knowledge of diamonds or any plastic or ceramic steel alloys. What is more, spectrographs have found remains of copper in the grooves

of diorite, which is equivalent to coming across a cork knife which shows signs of having sliced through a brick.

Did they harden the copper to inconceivable degrees? Did they soften the diorite until it turned into a kind of talc stone? We have no evidence in this respect, except for the spectrographic analyses mentioned above.

Similarly, immensely heavy blocks were placed on top of one another with extraordinary precision and their cracks sealed with quick-setting plaster, which indicates that they were moved by an enormous force, of which only the most powerful modern cranes might just be capable, or perhaps not, given the number of blocks and the time taken to set them in place.

It is tragicomical to recall the Japanese expedition which a few years ago made a miniature pyramid, 10 metres high, with one-ton blocks using the cranes of palm-tree trunks which appear in the explanatory diagrams of how the Egyptians built their pyramids... But the attempt had to be abandoned half-way through, because so many of the trunks kept splitting and showering the enterprising engineers with splinters.

Once again Egypt offers us its mysteries... synonymous with its name.

But... is there "another history" of Egypt and consequently of Thebes?

Not exactly, but there are traditions which can serve as possible alternatives... or no less impossible than those offered by official science. It is now time to look at these.

THE "OTHER HISTORY"

According to the old traditions, preserved in a number of highly fragmented documents from both East and West in the form of "Mythologies" or stories, like those recorded in the conversations which Plato held with the Egyptian priests, the Earth has been populated by men for millions of years.

These traditions show us a kind of "Proto-history" in which Cultures and Civilizations appear as mere instants in an immensely long and varied process of development. If this were true, what we know, or think we know, of the human past would be a negligible part of that past. According to Plato, the Egyptians told him how the earliest Athenians had conducted themselves admirably in sustained conflicts with the pirate fleets from the *Island of Poseidonis,* the last remnant of the Atlantean continent. Plato answered them that the Athenians knew nothing of this event which according to the Egyptians had occurred some ninety-five centuries

before; that is, a little over 11.800 years ago. To that display of ignorance, the priest answered with benevolent irony: "You Greeks will always be children."

More or less the same thing happened to the credulous Herodotus when the Egyptian priests told him of records being kept over a period of 17,000 years.

We can see now that our "scepticism" is not new... nor our ignorance either.

Coming back directly to our subject, the traditions tell us of that Atlantean continent which existed during an earlier stage of the cycle of Civilizations and Stone Ages, equivalent to the Middle Ages between two Civilizations. About 850,000 years ago, enormous cataclysms (which some sources attributed partly to the

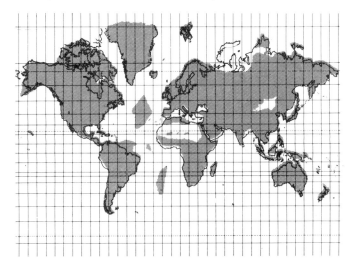

Possible marine contour lines, just before the last sinking movement of Atlantis (9650 B.C aprox)

uncontrolled use of *Marmash* or atomic energy which was derived from the conversion of energy into matter the reverse of the process which we are familiar with today) profoundly altered the face of the planet and the inclination of its axis in relation to the plane of the Ecliptic. The Great Atlantis split into two sub-continents, Ruta and Daitya for the Hindus. The shift of the Earth's axis caused the emergence of the Andes, America and part of Europe as we know them today.

As a result, Mankind was almost totally destroyed. Of those who were left, many lapsed into a barbaric "primitivism", and a few others inhabited the remains of the high cities. After a long period which it is not relevant to mention here, we encounter, some seven hundred centuries ago, the last remnant of Atlantis in the form of the Island of Poseidonis as described by Plato and which, apparently, had colonies in other parts of the world. Its advanced culture and civilization took root in Africa, in what would now be Upper Egypt, when the Nile, much shorter than it is now, flowed out without a delta in the environs of present-day Asyut, into the now vanished *Sahara Sea* whose waters surrounded what we know today as the Gizeh plateau, like a sacred island.

These Atlanteans established themselves in the area of Thebes around two main centres: one administrative and religious on the very site of the city which the Greeks were later to call Thebes; and the other at the more initiatic location of Abydos, which brought together the mysterious worshippers of a Holy Sepulchre, later to be called the Sepulchre of Osiris.

On the plateau they erected at least one Great Pyramid (two, according to other versions), bringing materials from the South and from other islands, on

one of which part of the city of Cairo stands today. This Pyramid was never a tomb, but a synthetic body of knowledge expressed through the medium of measurements and their relationships.

Many millenniums passed, and they built another great monument, partly making use of a natural sacred mound: the Great Sphinx, with its wings and a disk of burnished gold on its forehead designed to cast the reflection of the Sun's first rays between its paws, which were to be rebuilt so many times and which then extended their claws over the low cliff above the sea. This construction was a representation of the Four Elements in the form of Bull, Lion, Eagle and Man. There were numerous underground labyrinths leading off from the monument. There were passages and crypts dug out under the entire plateau, and it is said that one of these passages led as far as what is today the Red Sea, then a fertile valley which was later dedicated to the Mother of the World, known in the actual Egyptian period as Hathor or *House of Horus*, the concave allcontaining Space, with its two Principles: Nur representing Space, and Nut, the Starry or manifested Sky.

The face of the Sphinx, so many times remodelled, originally represented one of the great Magician-Kings of Atlantis.

Further convulsions and cataclysms raised the bed of the Sahara Sea (as we can call it in order to situate it in the reader's mind) and caused the submergence of major land masses in the North of Europe. The progressive disintegration of Atlantis and the transformations on the North American continent began increasingly to break up parts of land which had formerly been joined together and caused numerous islands

◀ *Page 38*
  Gizeh plateau. At the far end it
  can be seen the Nile's Valley

39

to sink. The River Nile was diverted into disease-ridden swamps, and for thousands of years the Gizeh plateau lay abandoned. But the powerful current of water gradually built a course for itself with its own mud across the marshes·which dried up and became deserts, and the river brought prosperity to its banks. For that reason, it had been known since time immemorial as *Hapi*, Happiness or He who brings happiness.

About 12,000 years ago or a little less, the last portion of the Atlantean continent disappeared in the mids of a cataclysm, though it had previously transferred most of its libraries and a few objects to the African colony: Egypt.

A wave of migration from the also disturbed region of Southern Asia reached Egypt, then called the Land of Kem (the dark, the burnt), revitalising the already large city of On, later called Was and finally Thebes. Its outskirts and many cities along the Nile likewise flourished. The Asiatic cobra entered Africa and was to become the symbol of the new unification, the *Uraeus or Uras*.

The Cult of the Sun (Ra) and the Spiritual Light (Amon) spread throughout the now independent ex-colony of Atlantis and one or two more pyramids, sanctuaries and temples were built. The Sacred Ways linked the early sanctuaries, which were gradually turning into theological complexes, like the one which was later to exist at Thebes, with a length of about 11km, and which linked what is today called the Temple of Luxor with the Temple of Karnak and those dedicated to Sekhmet. The subterranean part of the Holy Sepulchre of Osiris was completed with its *Osirions* dug deep down in.the rock and in galleries where the *99 Names of God*

were displayed, a tradition which was to be taken up in recent times by the Islamic religion. Just as the *Eye of Allah* is none other than the old *Eye of Horus*, an effective protection against spells.

A long series of 'Mythical Dynasties'' would then have succeeded one another, like that of King Oxyrrhinchus, King Scorpion, etc. Thus, by the time of the sinking of the Island of Poseidonis, which is the one which Plato specifically refers to, the Land of Kem was already highly organized and ready to receive the *Fire of Civilization*.

Stele known as that of King Serpent
Louvre Museum. Dynasty I

After the Mythical Dynasty of King Horus, between the 9th and 7th millennium BC, when the bed of the Eastern Mediterranean had been raised in several sections and when the waters had converted the fertile valley into the Red Sea, there arose the Dynasty of Menes or Narmer, which was to give a "modern" form to the Egyptian Empire.

Meanwhile there were tribes in the surrounding areas living at different stages of cultural development, and among those focal points we can find the ones which are today supposed to have given rise to Egypt. These tribes either became gradually assimilated to the Empire or else emigrated towards Central Africa, where some are still to be found in the same state of involution.

On an old sanctuary dedicated to the Sacred Bird the city of Memphis was built; but a remarkable fact commands our attention: the figure of Menes or Narmer, on the famous palette, wears the White Crown of Upper Egypt. For it was from Thebes that the new unification arose, althouh *the City of the White Wall,* Menphis, was to occupy a preponderant position over the coming millenniums, by uniting the White Crown with its Red one.

Ka statue of King Hor. Cairo Museum. New Kingdom

42

We have tried to draw from astronomical and astrological references what is strictly related to what we could call "History", if there were sufficient evidence to prove it all true. There then follow what are commonly known as the "Historical Dynasties" to which we have already referred, though in all honesty there is even in these much that is mythical or symbolic; especially in what has come to be called the Archaic Period, in which one of the Pharaohs bears the mysterious name of *Ka* or *The Double* (today we would say *Astral)*, and the period of the Old Kingdom (3rd Dynasty), in which another is called *Kabah,* of similar though not identical meaning.

The so-called *Father of History*, Herodotus, who was more like the first known "journalist", produced a number of real facts like the existence of the pygmies, and also several fantasies like the one about the men with an eye in the middle of their chests. The claims he makes in his sometimes frankly hilarious accounts about Egypt have unfortunately been taken by modern specialists as dogmas of faith.

We have given this bare picture of what tradition has to say about the origins of Egypt and of Thebes, its unifying heart in the early times, in order to balance the previously offered version, which was taken from the common denominator of modern historians.

Now the reader has two versions.

Both cannot be true, since they contradict one another on many points. Both could be false, although there are common elements which make one suspect the opposite. What is most likely is that there is an element of truth and falsehood in both of them... as in all things

in life. Let each one choose what his culture, his imagination and his intuition dictate.

The sages of antiquity used to say that nothing is totally true or totally untrue, and that this is what makes the Wheel of the Worlds go round.

UNITY BEHIND PLURALITY

According to Plato, the Empire of Atlantis had, besides its capital, colonies which he mentioned as being nine in number. Its emperor received the generic name of Atlas and with his associate Kings made up an Empire governed by the Laws of Poseidon, although they each retained a certain independence. Every five, six or seven years they or their representatives assembled to coordinate the whole. We have seen how a part of that whole was early Egypt, with its nucleus in the Theocracy of Thebes.

When the Atlantean Empire was destroyed, what we call Egypt today retained that style of plurality strongly permeated by a sense of *Transcendent Unity*. Present-day man, with his dialectical vision of the Universe and himself, has difficulty in conceiving that plurality-unity since he sees these concepts as opposites. With this mentailty, we would never be able to understand the Egyptian phenomenon, either materially or spiritually, and with all the varying shades in between.

But the Egyptian conception of things was by no means chaotic. It was based upon harmonic relationships between the different parts and upon a *Harmony* which gave them their being and which was before, behind and after all differentiation, past, present and future.

Its world was not stereotyped but rested in a perfectly balanced equilibrium, dynamic yet immutable, at least within an immense cycle of space-time.

The most basic example of this is the very location of Thebes. *The City* - which is how they referred to it, as was later also the case with Athens, Alexandria, Rome or Constantinople - was at the same time the image of the small and personal, of the limits which the human being needs to escape from the anguish of feeling lost in the cosmos, and of the greatness and universality which can contain all things, with the certain presentiment of an *other world* which is far above death and life. Far beyond anything that we humans can grasp with our reason.

Faluas.
Small boats
used on the
Nile for
transport

Thebes lay astride the Nile and extended along its two banks, with one as the mansion of the living and the other as the place of the dead.

The Nile, in turn, flowed through it, running almost exactly from South to North, and the Sun cruised above it with its shining disk, from East to West. From the place where one might watch the dawn, the tumult of a megalopolis could be heard in all its varied expressions, ranging from the mother rocking a cradle newly made for her offspring, to markets and squares always bustling with pedestrians and officials. In the architectural religious complex which was at once apart from and yet firmly a part of that human society of young people - for they tended to die soon after the age of thirty - other men and women, most of them also young, worked for the Invisible and for the visible in the most grandiose setting of enormous polychrome buildings which has ever to our knowledge been designed.

The "funerary" aspect presented today by the ruins of those temples and buildings, when observed by a tourist's eye which considers three or four days sufficient to visit them, did not exist. Today we see the bones of what was once a beautiful body, full of life, where art and the sciences had reached peaks so high that scholars will be astounded when they finally interpret them; for although now they are there to be seen, they do not see them.

The pharaoh was not called by his name, but by that title which can be approximately translated as *The inhabitant of the Great House,* just as Horus, the Falcon-God, is the inhabitant of the Great Cosmic House of Hathor.

Page 48 ▶
Decorating a wall using the fresco technique

But that Great House was very far from what we might imagine today as the house of a Sacralized Emperor, who believed and felt himself to be - and perhaps was - the blood, or rather, spiritual descendant of the Gods who had dwelt on the Earth in the First Times. It was merely a comfortable mansion, with spacious rooms and large gardens and ponds. Multicoloured awnings veiled even from the birds its mysterious yet happy privacy.

Attended like a God by a special priestly Brotherhood who dressed him ritually as the Sun rose over the horizon, and thus enabled him to reproduce all the natural and astronomical phenomena, he was the Lord of Life and Death over all. But at the same time he himself was more of a slave than any of his subjects, bound as he was to a ritual which by its immemorial antiquity had become natural and was performed with joy.

It is curious to behold the amazement felt by those who today look into the little that we know of Ancient Egypt and come up against the very strict rituals. They see them as an artificial mechanization of life, as a kind of absurd torture... And next moment they are chewing their food, closing their eyes when they go to sleep, making love or crying or laughing exactly as their ancestors did millions of years ago, following an unchanging ancestral ceremony. Why does everything have to change? This hypothesis born in the 18th-19th centuries is absurd. When the highest possible perfection has been reached, any change is decadence and inefficiency.

The so-called *Harem of Amon* had nothing to do with the present concept, a mixture of Islamic polygamy

◀ *Page 49*
Triad of Mykerinus. Cairo Museum
Dynasty V

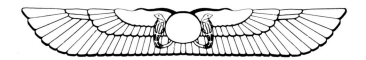

and European brothel. The polygamy that was accepted by many peoples of the world owes its existence to the fact that, in those fundamentally warlike races, the proportion of men in relation to women is very low, and if it were not considered legal and even obligatory for every man to take several wives and concubines, these would be condemned to live without the basic protection of the family nucleus. Prostitution, in the West, on the other hand, exists for socio-economic reasons, as a result of the destruction of the family, unemployment or badly paid work. The case of a prostitute being content with her profession is exceptional.

The *Harem of Amon* was formed by Princesses of royal blood and by the official Queen. The life they led was more akin to that of priestesses than anything else. In their mysterious meditations they had to become one with the Spirit of the Mother of the World, so that He-who-moves-the-fans - the Spiritual Wind of Amon - could, in a Sacred Union, in which it is said that even the sceptres and the ritual furniture took on life, effect the fertilization of the Queen or her Princesses by the Paharaoh. This ensured the physical perpetuation of the inheritance of the Kingdom through a genetic channel which, in those times, was the vehicle of all legal and actual continuity of Power.

Of course, alternatives had been considered for the very rare cases of infertility. At the turning-points of its History or when revolutions shook Egypt in its many thousands of years of existence, the Myth of Horus - who had replaced his dead Father in order to engender the manifested World with his Mother to bring to life an image of Himself to protect mankind - was applied

by analogy, and the renewal of the Dynasty or its
replacement by another was effected.

But there was a single moment during the year for
this encounter that would bring the Heir to light to take
place, when the astrological conditions were at their best
and the Priests had evoked the Soul which was to rein-
carnate as the one who would then be Pharaoh, Lord
of Upper and Lower Egypt, known by his first title as
Son-of-the-Sun. In case of necessity, other moments
would be used, but never would these be outside the
immemorial ritual norms which had proved, by the few
times they had been broken, their continued effec-
tiveness.

The Great House of the Pharaoh was almost entirely made of wood, and this wood was selected and
blessed. Some of it belonged to the Empire, while some
came from its remotest confines, like the cedars of
Lebanon. Or stones, like the red sandstone from Syria.
Doors, ceilings, walls, ponds, furniture, everything, absolutely everything had a ritual name, and the inhabitant of the Great House and his attendants had to know
the secret name of all that they touched.

The Pharaoh had to spend a considerable part of
the year travelling throughout his Empire and
sometimes, in warlike attire and surrounded by tamed
lions and vultures, make war at the head of his armies.
Another of his tasks was, surrounded by his
domesticated baboons, to pick mandrake, the symbol
of a certain curative magic, or with his large trained cats
(today this race of cats has died out, the most similar
being the Siamese), to hunt the goose, symbol of matter and of vanquished foes. His guard, like that of the

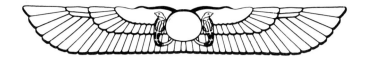

great temples dedicated to Amon, was not only made up of men, but of lions by day and black panthers by night.

Goose hunt. Tomb of Nakht, Theban necropolis. Dynasty XVIII

Of all the Sacred Festivals that the Pharaoh had to attend, the one which we can best understand in these times of euphoria for all things social is the one in which he was presented with huge round loaves of bread stamped with ansate crosses or keys of life. For about 24 hours the Pharaoh broke the loaves and the officials then reduced them to crums... as many as there were inhabitants in the Empire, according to the latest census, which he had been presented with by his specializ-

ed priests. Then, from boats and along roads, these tiny pieces of bread which had touched the Pharaoh's hands were scattered among all his subjects. Even the furthest inhabitant had the right to one, and if anyone should be left without his piece of sacralized bread, it could cost even the highest officials in the Administration their lives.

This Festival took place, like all the rest, once a year. And, like the Sacred Union which we mentioned above, it was performed in a Temple.

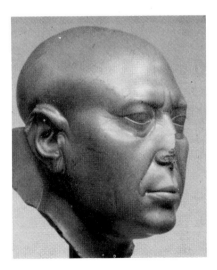

"Green head".
Representation
of an elder or priest
from the Ptolemaic
Epoch

On account of the secrecy that logically surrounded them, there is very little that can be said about the real Regents of Egypt, the Priests. We are not referring to the humble priests which every settlement had, who attended to the sick and dying, to births and

burials; and who knew everything from basic medicine to the principles of crop cycles, and of the construction of boats and household talismans. But to those at the summit of the Theocratic Pyramid.

It is useful to clarify that, owing to the high level of religious feeling among the Egyptian people, the beneficial absence of foreigners and even to certain mechanical and chemical contraceptives, the population of the Empire remained more or less stable for thousands of years. We can estimate it at about twelve million souls. Rigorous censuses were carried out every five or seven years, varying with the epochs.

While Thebes was the Capital, boats sailed from it every year with the Pennants of Amon and travelled all the way down the known and colonized Nile, bearing a high-ranking Priest. At each village they passed through, if the omens were propitious, the golden boat landed and the Priest or one of his high assistants descended, and chose, out of the children who had been born that year, one, at least, who would be taken to the boat so that on its return to Thebes he could enter on to the first rungs of the Sacerdotal School. The village thus honoured would celebrate with a holiday and the family of the chosen child attained considerable social standing.

Those chosen then began in Thebes a long "course of selection" according to the aptitudes they displayed. The majority entered into service at the Temples or at the Nobles' and Pharaoh's palaces. The rest, according to their natural inclinations, were sent to a Centre of Initiation where they specialized as doctors, scribes, archivists, soldiers etc. The most capable were promoted to the School of Amon itself. Very few attained to be

Priests or Priesteses of the God, taking on the vacant posts at the peak of the Theocratic Pyramid which, as the Imperial council and College of Magicians, maintained the Sacred Union between the terrestrial Egypt and the Celestial.

From what we know of it, the course of discipleship was extremely hard, the sacrifice of material life to the spiritual, total. In return, at a fixed time, they were branded on the left shoulder (not to be confused with the ritual tattoos which appear on the skin of mummies) at the front and back, by a pair of ritual tongs, with the symbol of the Uraeus Serpent which rendered them immune to any attack and guaranteed them complete safety within the Empire, regardless of the conditions in which they might find themselves... That strip of skin was removed when they died, to be carefully kept in certain special archives which had the function of "batteries" which magically charged the secret crypts of the temples.

Life in Thebes, *The City,* was rich and exultant, yet at the same time peaceful. It is very difficult, for a person of the 20th century, to conceive how people lived there, since the preconceptions proper to our age cast an impenetrable veil before our eyes and prevent us from understanding so different a way of life. Perhaps the most outstanding and remarkable feature we can point to is the lack of resentment among the citizens since, in spite of their large number (Thebes may have had more than 90,000 inhabitants), they managed to remain like a large family, with the special psychology of that lasting social nucleus which the family is. This does not mean that there were no problems; there have always been good people and bad people in

◀ Page 56
    Scribe from the Louvre.Painted lime
    stone statue with encrusted eyes

57

every age and there is no system that can restrain wicked natures or corrupt good ones; but a discipline, at once natural and practical and swiftly executed, maintained a harmonious order which made thefts, murders and assaults veritable exceptions that confirmed the rule of peaceful coexistence.

Far from the ''cliches'' with which our History books present us, the Theban was a cheerful and uncomplicated person.

Very skilful and efficient in everything he did, cheerfulness accompanied him, and if not, sadness or despair but very openly expressed. The affected intellectual, the critic of everything that others think and do, would have been seen as an extraordinary and even amusing phenomenon.

For those ancient inhabitants of The City, life and death, as they are now conceived, did not exist, and the grief which they experienced at the decease of their loved ones was similar to what today we might feel at the permanent departure of a beloved person who sets out on a long journey. Their faith in the fact that God and the Gods had made the World in the best possible way, saved them from any existential anguish, although it did not diminish their sensitivity, kindness and nostalgia, pervaded by a feeling of ultimate certainty in a destiny protected by a Universal Order that was just and good.

In Egypt there were no slaves; at most, prisoners of war condemned to labours outside the cities and frequently repatriated. Those who worked on the erection of an Obelisk did so as the Christian worked on the building of a Cathedral or the Moslem on that of a Mosque.

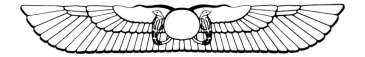

One modern criticism that tends to be made of the ancient Egyptians is that they clung to the mortal flesh, since they performed a complex rite of mummification in order to preserve the body.

Burial from the late predynastic period. 3300BC British Museum

Those who are familiar with the climate of Egypt know that such funerary operations were not aimed at keeping the body intact, since merely by burying them in the parched soil of the west bank, they would have been preserved - as modern Archaeology has shown - in better conditions than after a process of mummification. Moreover, this psychopompic process was strictly reserved for the Pharaohs, the Nobles, the Priests and for those who had distinguished themselves in their service to the community. Only in the times of decadence, with the advent of the Plutocracy which finally corrupted the original Theocracy, were the funerary opera-

tions placed within the reach of anyone who could pay for them, regardless of his spiritual condition. But that was one of the many side-effects of foreign infiltration and of the decline of the old customs. Just as Egypt had taken a long time to be born, so it also took a long time to die, and the Land of Magic par excellence eventually became, in Roman times, the principal granary for Europe. On the disintegration of that immense Theocratic State, its already crumbling monuments and its knowledge of nature and the Soul astounded the world and were stimulants to new spiritual adventures, from that of Greece to Islam. But the Great Mysteries returned to the Source of Grace from which they had come, awaiting the advent of more propitious times.

We have already mentioned that as the New Kingdom was losing its driving *impulse*, after the Ramesid dynasties, the centuries were employed by the last Priest-Magicians in gathering up and hiding away everything from their knowledge to the ritual objects, except for those which on account of their great size had to be abandoned to their fate, once almost all of them had been deactivated. And those which were not deactivated await, like the Great Sleeper, safe from the curiosity of those alien to the *things of mystery* (even though some of them are physically visible to millions of visitors), the moment of the *inexorable cyclic resurrection* of the Sacred Times.

We have written something about the Thebes of the Living and now we shall do the same for that other Thebes, that of the Dead, which flourished on the West Bank, that of the Setting Sun, Maamon, in the historical period of Thebes. It was not its antithesis but the complement (or vice versa) of the other side of the River

of Visible Life: *Hapi, Happiness, the Blue, the River-
that-descends-from-Heaven,* the stream of divine Breath
laden with gifts, which unites the far-scattered villages
and reflects on Earth another river of stars which runs
across the Sky and which the Sun must cross, like the
Gods, like Man.

To the West, about eight kilometres from the river,
behind the hills of Deir-El-Bahari, lies the so-called
Valley of the Kings, at the head of a long gorge or
depression which the natives of today define as Wadi-
Biban-El-Moluk, that is, the Valley of the Gates of the
Kings. This valley has two entrances, that of the East
and that of the West, and today is a desert although
it was not in antiquity, when the Red Sea was a fertile
valley. At that time, this and other similar valleys which
lie alongside it were fertile, and prehistoric hunters have
left drawings on their rocks which depict them giving
chase to elephants and ostriches. Beyond this Valley rise
the great hills of the Western Mountain and the Gurn,
a peak which constitutes the highest point. If we cross
these geological undulations, so greatly altered today
both by erosion and by the work of man, we come upon
the immense desert, the former bed of the prehistoric
sea.

Likewise, in the environs of the Valley of the Kings,
lie the so-called Valley of the Queens and Valley of the
Nobles.

The whole area forms what look like natural am-
phitheatres where the relentless Sun is reflected and
makes the temperature rise, turning it into one of the
hottest places on the planet. It is hard to believe that
about ten thousand years ago, and even less, water danc-

Page 62 ▶
*The author in the Valley of the Kings at
the entrance to Tutankhamon's tomb*

61

ed in cascades through the woods, the temperature was agreeable and the region provided a home for a multitude of living beings.

Valley of kings. Access road

The Arabic name which refers to the *Gates of the Kings* suggests to us what the more intelligent historians are discovering: that the present atmosphere of desolation, accentuated by the successive excavations which, in certain places, make it look as if a heavy mortar bombardment has taken place, does not correspond to that which the Valley would have had in the 18th or 20th Dynasty. Several indications which had already been spotted by the titanic excavator Belzoni at the beginning of the 19th century, point to the fact that the tombs hewn from the rock, whose entrances are bare today, would once have been adorned with lavish decoration and had light-leafed wooden doors open during the day, as happens in the cemeteries of some countries today.

◄ *Page 63*
The author in front of one of the Colossi of Memnon. Valley of the Kings. Approach by road

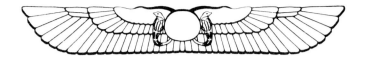

Or else, at other times of the year, they would have remained closed for ritual reasons.

In synthesis, in the other Thebes, that of the Dead, the Brotherhoods under the banner of the couchant jackal, which can still be seen on seals as a representation of the highly esoteric God Anubis, lived in particular parts of that City of the Dead and controlled the armed guards and trained animals who protected the treasures from the unremitting greed of the desert bandits.

Clay seal showing the stamp of the jackal lying on the nine captives. Tutankhamon's tomb.

It is possible that, like other ancient peoples, the Egyptians periodically assembled there to bring offerings to members of their families and to the Pharaohs, Nobles and Priests whose bodies reposed in the inaccessible depths of those subterranean Temples, the

"launching-pads" for the Souls of the good, whose relics had been consecrated in the same way that millenniums later other religions would do with their "saints", to whom they also attributed wonders and "miracles".

A transcendental sense of unity thus linked the two Thebes in complementary harmony.

A number of funerary Temples were likewise erected on the West Bank, as the colossal ruins of the Ramesseum and of the Temple of Hatshepsut demonstrate. There also are the enigmatic *Colossi of Memnon* dedicated to the Rising Sun. The birth, splendour and declination of the Sun were given the names of Memnon, Amon and Maamon, and death is birth and sunrise on the other shore of Life.

According to contemporary archaeologists, these figures of giants seated on their ritual thrones stood in

Collosi of Memnon. West Bank

front of the funerary Temple of Amonhotep III, of which they would be the only remaining testimony. Esoteric Tradition holds them to be much older than any edifice dedicated to an "historical" Pharaoh, and says that they were an offering to the Rising Sun, just as the simple, though not always unintelligent popular belief continues to call them.

Their present height is about eighteen metres, though it is probable that with their crowns and accountrements they may have risen to a few metres more. They were restored and reinscribed an infinite number of times. Celebrated in classical antiquity, there were musicians from Greece who made pilgrimages there in order to hear the seven primordial sounds which, at dawn, one of them clearly emitted. In Roman times there was mention of one note in particular, corresponding to the *fa* of our musical scale. The restorations of the Emperor Septimus Severus, in the year 199, silenced for ever the Colossus which had emitted that sound, situated to the North. One of the many explorers of the 19th century asserted at a London scientific soiree that he had heard that musical note once again, but there is no evidence for it, nor has it been proved by the exhaustive experiments carried out in the 20th century without any positive results. Official science explains the phenomenon (as we know, the present idiosyncracy consists in explaining everything away, whether or not the truth is known) by attributing it to the expansion of one of the rocks on being heated by the first ray of the Sun, after the coldness of the desert night. We cannot agree with this, since the imposing mass of the Colossus in question makes it impossible for the Sun to bring about any appreciable rise in temperature in the cool dawns, even on one of the outer stones. We believe that the

enigma remains intact, like the two colossal monuments, though, like them, damaged by the violent ignorance and vanity of men.

A great effort is needed to imagine that Thebes of the dead as it was some 3000 or more years ago, for since the Thebes of the Living, with its gardens and ponds, was almost totally destroyed, the climate has changed. Moreover, the lootings, demolition by explosives and excavations both ancient and modern, combined with natural silt deposits and the network of tourist routes, have radically altered the appearance of Western Thebes. The drawings made in the 18th century, in the 19th, and even the photographs from the beginning of the 20th, show us the latest great changes. What would the earlier ones have been like? Their

Interior of the tomb of Thothmes III. In the foreground the king's sarcophagus.

magnitude escapes us and we may each let our imagination fly wherever it will.

Perhaps owing to the temptation of the enormous treasures buried there, we have comparatively more historical information about the West of Thebes than the East. Its magical attraction has captivated millions of people from classical times to our own. In Memphis there existed another Valley of the Kings, but as the City of the White Wall was built mainly with bricks and with a far smaller supply of stone, very little has survived down to our own times. It is possible that in the classical epoch everything was already buried by the new constructions, since Memphis was inhabited until the end

Temple of Luxor. On the right, the mosque of Abu el Haggag.

of the Roman Empire and in one way or another never ceased to be lived in. Thebes, on the other hand, was abandoned, and the town of Luxor, of Arabic origin, was settled at a late date, when many constructions on

the East Bank were already protected by the sand, as is demonstrated by the Mosque which was built on the roof of the Temple of Luxor and by the marks left at a great height by Arabian knives being sharpened on the rocks of Temple walls throughout almost all of Upper Egypt.

In spite of the fact that many tombs may have been opened in the time of the Greeks and Romans, neither of these did any more than leave some superficial *graffiti* on the original stuccoes and paintings. Recently, some *graffiti* in demotic script have been found, which would mean that, in spite of the precautions of the Priests at the end of the New Empire to seal up and conceal the majority of the tombs, some remained open to popular devotion until the final epochs, from the 25th to the 30th Dynasties.

Watercolour showing the entrance to the Tomb of the Kings of Thebes as they appeared in the year 1850

Diodorus Siculus, in the 1st century BC, in his *General History,* includes this account which he claims to have heard in Thebes: "The Priests told me that in their records they find forty-seven tombs of Kings, but in the time of Ptolemy, son of Lagos, they say that only seventeen of these remained, many of which had already been destroyed when we visited those regions"

Strabo, in the age of the Emperor Augustus, some seventy years later, visited the Valley of the Dead with his friend, the Governor of Egypt, Elius Galus. He tells us: "Above the Memnonium (the Ramesseum or the Colossi?), in caves, are the tombs of the Kings, dug out of the rock. They are about forty in number, are wonderfully constructed, and make a sight worthy to be seen".

The Greeks had already given the buriel passages the name of syrinxes, since they reminded them of the musical instrument. And they also believed that in the Valley or in its proximity was the Tomb of Memnon, perhaps connected with the Colossi. Modern historians believe that they were referring to the great tomb of Rameses VI, but of this we have no evidence.

Over two thousand brief inscriptions written by tourists of the Roman and Byzantine epochs are preserved. There are poems and laudatory phrases of all kinds. The last of these correspond to the 8th century. All of the recorded inscriptions are in the great tombs of the 19th and 20th Dynasties, from which it can be deduced that they were open and easily accessible. It is probable that there are still many thousands of inscriptions that have not come to light, either because we have failed to see them or because they are still buried. It is curious

to find that the modern tourists who look upon the walls of those tombs never notice them. It is equally strange that the religious upheavals which followed the fall of the Roman Empire, and the appearance of thousands of Christian sects, some of which had succumbed to real madness (like that of Afu *the Buffalo* who went about on all fours amongst the animals, or Mary *the Egyptiac* who died confined in a mastaba or Egyptian tomb, having whitewashed it and surrounded her dwelling with

Temple of Hatshepsut. Back wall of the Chapel of Anubis. The figure on the left has been completely hammered away, as has the cartouche with his name and some hieroglyphics. Deir-el-Bahari. Thebes. Dynasty XVIII

her own waste, or Simon *the Stylite* who had his followers carry his own worms up to him on the high capital where he lived in order to be closer to God, and so many others who devoted themselves, "as an act of piety", to roaming the banks of the Nile with hammers and chisels to deface everything "pagan"), had little

effect on the tombs of the Valley. Christian communities are known to have lived in these tombs, and shown their guests the magnificent paintings as representations of hell made by the Devil in person, but they did not damage them and restricted themselves to writing pious and tender prayers on them in a quick and spontaneous manner.

These communities or community of early Christians have left traces of their existence in what to-day are remains of small churches beside the tombs of Rameses III and Rameses IV, re-using ancient materials. There are also remains of kitchen-ware with prayers carved on them, and a detail which has not yet been studied: shells of the fruit of the plant *balinites,* which is a hallucinogen. Did those simple believers in Christ have recourse to drugs, in order to achieve states of self-hypnosis which would enable them to obtain visions or hallucinations propitious to their faith? We do not know, but the wave of "religious madness" which spread over Egypt with the advent of the first Christians could well have given rise to unsuspected manifestations and excesses, mixed with a great naivete and childlike tenderness. The expedition of John Romer, an excellent archaeologist and a writer of fine sensitivity, found that the tomb of Rameses XI had been converted into a stable and also into a bedroom and kitchen; the ritual well was used as a dustbin and a Byzantine coin was found, together with remains of food which indicate that these pacific invaders did not observe any ritual diet, but fed themselves on red meat, fish, greens and grain, as well as rye bread.

All Egypt had passed into dependence on the Eastern Roman Empire, but Byzantium was still weak and was a long way away. So, when the Arab invasion

came in the year 639, in spite of the fact that the rising forces of Islam were numerically insignificant and not very well organized, they encountered no other resistance than the distances. For the "renowned general and consul, the most magnificent Patrician of the Empire, Theodosius", at that moment Governor of Egypt, collected the taxes and escaped with a small fleet from Alexandria, a city which was to be finally abandoned in the year 642. The Arabian general Amr Ibn-Al-As was later to write to the Caliph Omar, who was in Mecca, that he had taken the immense city without resistance and that he was annexing all Egypt to his Empire.

In one century, the Christian communities disappeared, were converted or emigrated to more distant places. The natives of Egypt had been morally and physically annihilated centuries before and thus the new masters entered the double Thebes, while the Valley of the Kings lay abandoned to the forces of Nature. The City became a quarry for Mosques and, uncared for, began to disappear beneath the sands.

Perhaps it has not been sufficiently explained that in Ancient Egypt the only imposing and solidly built constructions were the Temples and Pyramids. As we have seen, even the Palaces, not excluding the Pharaoh's, were built of precious but light and easily perishable materials; and as for the houses and huts of the people, they were made of unbaked bricks or simply of mud and reeds. It is known that in the annual flooding of the Nile many houses were destroyed and, with great rejoicing, their inhabitants erected new ones during a Festival which renewed the cycle of life, always the same and yet always different. The forces of the Spirit and of nature had combined to make of Ancient

Egypt a unique Empire, the like of which, as far as we know, has never existed on the Earth; although we suspect that the Mayas, in the other outflow of the Atlantean expansion, had similar characteristics, to judge by what has remained of them: only Temples and Pyramids.

Thus, the changes which it is necessary for us to mention in order to understand this singular phenomenon of the Civilization of Ancient Egypt, promoted in its people a cheerful and vital resignation at every swing of the pendulum of History.

Tribes of Bedouins and other nomads from the desert came to the fertile lands of the Nile, and there, under the rule of Moslem life, a new order began to be formed and a new, though comparatively tepid awakening.

Modern Arabs on the outskirts of Thebes. In the background a typical mud hut can be seen

For the Europeans, Thebes became another of those remote cities which belonged to vanished ages, like the legendary Troy. The Bible and the works of Homer and of the Roman classics were the only survivors of those heroic times and, in some way, the prophecy which the Christians had proclaimed about the *end of the world* had come true. As for the Moslems who, though they were at that time in full expansion, are also erroneously placed in the Middle Ages - for it was no Middle Ages for them - they reactivated commerce, which arose initially from the lootings. The paved roads of the Egyptian Empire disappeared to give way to the caravan routes and the Nile continued to be the principal means of communication.

In the age of the Crusades, some Christians confused the great Pyramids with the *Granaries of Abraham*, while the Light-house of Alexandria, one of the Seven Wonders of the Ancient World, had collapsed as a result of an earthquake and of the excavations which had been made into its foundations by all kinds of adventurers in search of treasures. As we have already said, the Caliph Omar had ordered the last remains of the Library of Alexandria to be burnt, and the great city lingered on as a commercial and military port, and its palaces were dismantled in order to build Cairo, as well as mosques and new palaces, there or in distant cities. Several canals and ramifications of the Nile silted up, and others were opened, while the Delta became wider and almost entirely divested of its former vegetation and fauna.

Thebes, with its immense quadrilateral still visible from an aeroplane flying at an altitude of over 5000 metres, became reduced to the citadel of Luxor. The Valley was forgotten, except by the looters, although

even they now scarcely had access to the tombs owing to alluviums and rockfalls. Many Temples on the outskirts of Thebes were brought back into use, by placing planks of wood between their columns - something which caused considerable damage - as stables and stopping - places for the caravans. The smoke from the fires and that produced by the burnt fat of roasted meat progressively obscured the multi-coloured ceilings and walls. As we have said, the walls which stood out above he sands and mountains of debris served to sharpen knives or to form the foundations of mosques.

There was no lack of self-seeking individuals who tunnelled into the Pyramids and were ever in search of treasures, destroying the precious sarcophagi of sycamore and cedar when they discovered that they were not made of gold; those which were made partly of precious metals were also destroyed in order to melt down those riches. Mummies were used to manure the earth, and not only in Egypt, for up until the 19th century they were imported from Europe to make magical medicines, and those of cats and fish were used in Great Britain as fertilizers.

With the fall of Constantinople and with the retreat of the Arabs throughout the Mediterranean basin after the famous battle of Lepanto, a number of learned Moslem and later Christian travellers visited the ruins of Thebes. But even in the 19th century there were few who recognised anything of what they saw. A just exception can be made in the case of the Jesuits, since we know that the fathers Protias and Francois covered Thebes thoroughly and made drawings and measurements of great merit. They also visited the Valley of the Kings, although in the end they were

unable to correlate the accumulated material and could not state categorically that this was in fact the ancient *Thebes of the Hundred Gates*. Later in 1707, the Jesuit Claude Sicard, assigned to a Mission in Cairo, was sent by the King of France himself to travel up the River Nile and draw up plans with notes on the great ruins. It seems that he got as far as Aswan and Philae, and with the books of Strabo and Diodorus of Sicily in his possession was able to locate with certainty Thebes and its Necropolis, of which he left a precise description, counting ten accessible tombs which had impressed him. Many of his papers reached France and extracts were published in Jesuit newspapers. He died in Cairo during the plague of 1726, and part of his valuable material was lost, but he may still be considered as the discoverer of Thebes after a millennium of uncertainties.

His work awakened the curiosity of his contemporaries. According to an inscription now disappeared or lost, carved on a tomb, another clergyman, Richard Pococke, would have been in the Valley of the Kings on the 16th of September 1739. The published work of Pococke has the great novelty of including a detailed map of the Valley and the location of its tombs, although some of them were never found. In 1790 five thick volumes by James Bruce were published, containing an extraordinary work on Egypt. He had made the journey in 1768 and his book included a section on the old city of Thebes with its two settlements, on either side of the river. He had made an engraving of the tomb of Rameses III with two harpists, probably blind, which so moved the romantically-minded, that it later became known as *The Tomb of Bruce*.

At the end of the 18th century a number of excavations were carried out, which are now difficult to place

exactly, but which at the time received the general name of *the Turkish excavations,* due to the fact that Egypt had become a part, albeit a rather remote one, of the remains of the Turkish Empire.

We have to wait for the mysterious campaign of Napoleon (at the beginning of the 19th century), with his army accompanied by numerous scientists, draughtsmen and literati, to have a reliable source of what then remained of Ancient Egypt. And I venture to denominate this military campaign of the *Great Corsican* as "mysterious" since, apart from the military objective of cutting off Britain's communications with

Napoleon in front of a Pharaoh's mummy after the taking of Alexandria

India, one can sense an enigmatic inclination in the future Emperor of Europe towards Egypt, who went so far as to confess that it was not the first time he had

been there. Was he perhaps referring to some previous incarnation? Or simply to a rather unlikely secret journey? We shall never know for certain, but his beliefs and his parapsychological powers, educed in a number of battles in which he was actually seen in seven different places at once, lead us to suspect that he was frequently troubled by certain reminiscense. His respect and attraction for the Sacred Places was remarkable, so much so that he insisted on visiting Bethlehem in spite of all the dangers involved.

No sooner had the Mamelukes been deposed, in the three years or so that the French occupation of Cairo lasted, than an enormous transformation came about in the old Land of Kem. In Napoleon's own words, he was there to "help Egypt go towards the Light". And the fact is that he achieved this, for he founded scientific institutes, had maps drawn up, commissioned masterly drawings of the colossal ruins, unearthed the

Reconstruction of the Denderah Zodiac

Sphinx once more from the sands and even ordered one of its shoulders to be drilled through in search of the passages referred to in ancient times. At Denderah he made the gesture, never to be repeated by a conqueror, of leaving an exact replica of the great stone of the Zodiac, before having the original transported to Paris, His scientists recognised the importance of the trilingual Rosetta Stone, which by pacts of war passed into the possession of Great Britain, although it was to be the Frenchman Champollion who, working from copies, discovered the means of reading the old hieroglyphics.

Napoleon's work in Egypt was of such intensity that his achievements ranged from the modernization of hospitals to the drawing and description of the flowers of Nubia. The French presence in the domain of science outlasted the British domination, and still lingers on in these final decades of the 20th century.

One of Napoleon's great scientists, Denon, made the first "scientific" description of the Valley of the Kings and of a small village established there which he called Gurna; such was his enthusiasm that he generally used to go on ahead of the army of occupation in spite of his approaching old age and obesity. The Valley which he saw was not the same as the one that we see now, since the excavations and widening of the roads which are used by the millions of tourists have changed everything. But his accounts give us an idea of the almost sacred impulse which moved those men and of how much closer they were, with their sacralized Napoleon, with their readings of the Classics in Greek and Latin, with their long treks by boat, on horseback or on foot, with their sleeping in tents or in decaying Arabian palaces, to the ancient Egyptians, than we

researchers, living at the end of the 20th century, can ever be. The colourful troops, the rhythmic beating of the drums, the highly stratified but at the same time profoundly human way of life, the knowledge of the Classics at first-hand, placed them in special contact with old Egypt.

Allegorical portrait of Baron Denon

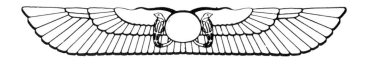

Today, our cameras can photograph or film in a few seconds what used to take a good draughtsman days; our hurry to reach nowhere in particular or simply because we·have to count the notes or travellers' cheques that we have in our pockets; our "democratic" sense which makes us accept as normal that people should wander through the Sanctuaries in shorts; our fear of Nature which, at the first hint of darkness, makes us take refuge, in the best of cases, in the hotels of modern-day Luxor, inevitably deprive us of that contact. We ought to reflect on these things before launching into criticisms of the comprehensible failings of those pioneers.

Not long ago I visited in London, in a small museum which until a short time ago was private, the sarcophagus of Seti I, a phenomenal piece of alabaster carved with hieroglyphics filled in with blue cobalt which have unfortunately deteriorated because of the London climate. It was brought to Europe, like so many other masterpieces, by the almost superhuman Belzoni, who also made extraordinary drawings, in colour of the now dilapidated tomb of Seti I, which exceed the possibilities of modern photography. To illustrate the value of these old techniques, we have published the drawing made by Bonomi of the bottom of the Sarcophagus. Moreover, in 1821, in Piccadilly, London, Belzoni had reproduced the tomb of Seti I in an extraordinary archaeological-artistic venture which still astounds us today.

Many other works and discoveries were carried out by this pioneer who is so much criticized today by archaeologists, since his methods, like those of Schliemann at Troy, were not entirely adequate or "scientific". But

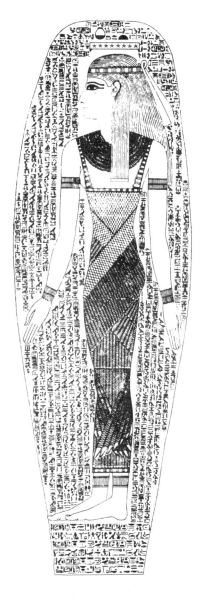

Drawing by Joseph Bonomi of the bottom of the alabaster coffin of Seti I

let us not forget that thanks to those "antique dealers" who found enormous historical treasures "by chance", we possess the most beautiful specimens of our Museums and many minute descriptions, made at the cost of unthinkable sacrifices, of paintings from the Valley of the Kings which have now disappeared at the hands of *souvenir*-hunters or dealers of all nationalities.

Facade of the Cairo Museum

So a great many of those remains have ended up in private collections and museums with inadequate means at their disposal for conservation? True. But it is also true that in the store-rooms of the great "Official Museums" thousands of precious objects lie rotting under piles of others, and that there are a great many display cases in the Museum of Cairo itself which have not been opened or cleaned once in the last 50 years, and that irreplaceable papyri are disintegrating

because of being mounted in ancient cases from the epoch of Maspero, in which the glass no longer fits properly and which are exposed to the sun flooding through the large windows which either have no curtains at all or have curtains which do not work or which no one ever remembers to draw.

In other parts of the world, for example in Lima, Peru, it is absolutely forbidden to take even the smallest earthenware pot from the Pre-Columbian epoch out of the country, in order to protect the "National Heritage"... but each new earthquake smashes hundreds of vases which are piled up on top of one another in the Larco Herrera Museum; or again, because of being locked up in large huts without any security control, 10,000 huacos of silver, gold and metallic alloys have disappeared from the National Museum of Archaeology over the last ten to twenty years.

This is not an attempt to justify the more or less silly ambition of dealers and "nouveaux riches" who long to have an archaeological piece in their bedroom; we are merely taking the opportunity to point out that sometimes the "official museums" which are held in so much respect do not have the moral right to criticize anyone or lay down the law about anything. Sometimes, a feeling of affection for antiquities can count for more than high-sounding qualifications. And the great discoveries, both in the Valley of the Kings and at other sites around the world, were achieved by what we in our ignorance call "chance" or through the information of some illiterate peasant. The scientists, for all their brains, cannot attribute to themselves finds which they have only been able to make by taking advantage of the help of the humble inhabitants of the desert, whose

names we shall never know and which no book ever mentions. (There are countless examples of this... from the Venus de Milo to the Treasure of Tutankhamon, since Carter, prior to his scientific work and his recovery operation which is a masterpiece, received information which led him to the discovery.)

That tomb of the young Monarch of the 18th Dynasty was in fact the last important discovery in the Valley of the Kings. Are there new discoveries awaiting us in the future? It is quite possible, since the so-called Valley of the Kings and its adjoining valleys of the Queens and Nobles, were never a "cemetery" in the present sense of the term, but The Other Thebes, the great Necropolis, which was once much frequented and wonderful to behold. Lying at the foot of the Western Mountain it drew to itself much of the splendour of the last historical period of the *City of a Hundred Gates*. And the Final Mystery of the Secret Rites.

THE MYSTERY OF THE
INNER CONSTITUTION
AND NATURE OF MAN

The lives of all the peoples of antiquity were governed by an *Esoteric Teaching* on the inner constitution, visible and invisible, of the Universe and of Man.

The reason behind the great similarity that underlies all those ancient Civilizations is open to different interpretations; but if we choose to interpret it in the light of a Traditional Teaching which would be the result of a common origin for Mankind and an Instruction common to all peoples, we find that all of them considered Man as a part of Nature - and by part we do not mean a fragment, but an integral part which contributes to its wholeness and explains it. In this way we can shed a little light on what otherwise would seem to be a theological absurdity.

From old Thebes and from Egypt in general, we are going to take a few simple but illuminating elements.

Firstly we want to make it clearly understood that the ancient Mysteries were never widely accessible, but were controlled by Priestly Brotherhoods who had understood that the ordinary man needs exoteric religions, with simple teachings about rewards and punishments which recompense and penalise their actions. The Secret Teachings are extremely dangerous if they are approached with a simplistic vision; as a result, they were "translated" for the popular mentality according to the geopolitical and spiritual necessities of each age of Humanity.

Three types of Egyptian script: hieroglyphic, hieratic and demotic

Consequently, apart from an ethico-spiritual common denominator, the formal conceptions of a Greek are different from those of a Chinese, as those of a Maya are from an Egyptian's. Nor are they the same in the religions which survive today; the recommendations of a Hebrew, those of a Christian, a Buddhist or a Muslim are not the same in every respect. But if we go deeper, we will find what could be called some *Permanent Values* which are the same in all of them. These are no

different from those held by the ancient peoples or from those which, most probably, will inspire the peoples of the future. What is renewed is the presentation, for since men are volatile creatures who are still in a state of spiritual infancy, they need periodical changes of forms and colours in order to continue with the game of life.

When Moses had to convert a nomadic tribe into an irradiating centre of spiritual culture, he could hardly have given out an eclectic message, since the tribal mentality prevailing amongst the Israelites meant that they needed to feel separated from other nations in order to be united amongst themselves. In the case of Jesus Christ, in order to initiate a new way of life - what the early Church Fathers called a *New Man* - he had to promote a rejection of the excess of worldly power of the Roman Empire which, drunk with glory, had reached the point of worshipping itself, not as a means - in the Augustan manner of "For the Empire towards God", which he synthesized in his own title of Augustus, until then reserved solely for Jupiter - but as a mechanical cult of attributes above Being. Thus, his followers helped to bring about the disintegration of one world so that another might be born. To give one more example, Mohammed had to infuse into the explosive Arab people the cult of *Holy War,* the conquest of living space as an expression of spiritual space, while at the same time he prevented diseases, like trichinosis, by convincing them that the pig is an unclean animal.

The exoteric or popular religions have that double virtue: that of elevating man spiritually, irrespective of the means employed, and that of achieving a level of hygiene in their bodies and their minds.

The esoteric is different, if not in those Permanent Values mentioned above, certainly in its major concerns; for it works with small elite groups who are naturally prepared (whether one accepts reincarnation or the simple Grace of God) to approach deep subjects without their minds being unhinged at the sight and understanding of the so-called Mysteries.

In Egypt in general, and in Thebes in particular, the two extremes co-existed: an exoteric religion for the people which, without complicating their lives, offered happiness to the good or destruction to the bad, and a Priestly College which was dedicated to Sacred Research. What is truly remarkable is that in old Kem both systems somehow managed to exist side by side in an acceptable manner for thousands of years in a synchronization of innumerable shades and tints. Apart from the "heresy" of Akhenaten, there were never any major confrontations and even this one was short-lived.

Let us see how these Mysteries were reflected externally. We shall take as an example the *Sevenfold Constitution* of nature and Man.

If we accept the old principle that Man is the key to Nature - as Protagoras' aphorism, "man is the measure of all things" correctly reaffirmed - we shall begin with the conception of the School of Thebes about the constitution of Man.

From the text generally entitled *Book of the Dead* (so called because it was found in association with mummies, on murals, bandages of royal linen and papyri), but whose more correct name would be *Book of the Hidden Dwelling,* we have reproduced the version of the *Papyrus of Ani,* fortunately stored and magnificent-

Page 93 ▶
The weighing of the Heart. Papyrus of Ani.
British Museum. Dynasty XIX

ly displayed in the *British Museum,* in one of its later but clearer forms. In it the central position is occupied by a pair of scales, while beside it the jackal headed God, Anubis, the guardian and protector of the dead, is weighing the Heart of the deceased, to see whether it is as light as the Feather of Maat, Justice, which can be seen on the opposite dish. On the far right appears the God Thoth, who represents the Universal Law, Wisdom and the Art of Healing the living and the dead, in the form of a man with the head of an ibis bird; on a coloured board and with an ordinary brush he is writing down the details of the Judgement. Beside him is the Monster-which-devours-hearts, a representation of the Chaos into which the wicked fall. On the far left, the figure of a woman with the Sistrum of Isis, the Mother Goddess, accompanies another figure who symbolizes the Spirit of the one standing trial and who, in his pristine Presence has the same stature as the Gods.

We shall now proceed to a description of the different parts which go to make up man, represented in the papyrus with an educational clarity.

1) Directly below the cross-bar of the scales one can see a quadrilateral stone, which in reality is a flattened cube, crowned only by a human head. It is the CHAT or KHAT, the matter of the physical body, which in life was crowned by the head or intelligence, giving it human form. It is inert, a simple piece of matter, a "brick" in the Universe to which it returns in that form, as a simple raw material which once had a human appearance. It is the *Cubic Stone*, a description of which was to reach the Alchemists of the European Renaissance, in one of its keys.

2) Hanging from the far left of the cross-pole of

the scales, under the cords which form an upward-pointing triangle, one can see a red Jar or a Heart. It is the representation of the vital energy which gives movement to the physical body, or simply the life which the deceased lived. One of its several names in ANKH, which also corresponds with that of the Key of Life, the figure in outline of a man with an upside-down triangle for his head, which is sometimes painted in red to reinforce its sense of a communicating door between the visible and the invisible.

3) Between the above-mentioned dish of the scales which supports the Heart, and the vertical column of the instrument, we see a human figure which is the *Double*, the KA, seat of the feelings, vehicle of the Spirit made in its image, and which in turn gives its form to the physical body throughout its life. It is in a posture of movement because it is able to walk, move about like a luminous ghost, and can even vouch for Man himself when he is asking for justice. It appears before the Gods and also before men when its virtues could not attain the Paths of Heaven, and it was condemned to wander for a time over the Earth. We shall shortly see how in mummification measures were taken to prevent this from happening.

4,5) A pair of feminine human figures which, amongst others, receive the name of AB and BA. In the papyrus they are situated on the left of the dish of the scales which supports the Heart. Usually, one is shown naked while the other is clothed, or else one with a very simple costume and the other with a highly embroidered one. They are the two parts of the Human Mind: one higher, denuded of vanities, and the other lower, in close contact with the pluralities of manifesta-

tion. AB is that part made of complex structures where the ideas-desires originate, the seat of cunning and of speculating selfishness. BA is, on the other hand, the seat of the Pure Ideas, those which are able to rise above the things of the earthly world; it receives the Higher Light from its position of human smallness. It is the mental Self, the consciousness of individual existence. But human imperfection still keeps them together, close to one another, as if they were twin sisters. BA is the Hidden Place, the Chamber where one awaits the Spiritual Resurrection.

Tomb of Anurkaui. The deceased before the Phoenix of Heliopolis. Ramessid epoch

6) This Spiritual Resurrection is represented by a Bird - in the Theban figures a cross between a swallow and a falcon - with a human head. In Memphis it was represented by the Phoenix or Bird of Resurrection. One of its names, in Thebes, in AKHU or CHEYBI, and it symbolizes the Intuition of Sacred Things. In one key it is the Soul, the Shining Spiritual part which gives rise to White Magic, Marvels and Holy Acts. It has the property of being able to perch, as we see in the papyrus, on the roof of concrete things, and also, because of its bird-nature, to rise up and fly towards the heights of the *Other Land,* the *Magic Square* illuminated by Amon or the Spiritual Light. That *Other Land* is the Mansion of the Blessed, the Amenti, literally *The Land of Amon,* or better *The Country of Amon* or *The Great House of Amon*, which is perfect and stable.

7) Finally there is the large figure on the left, in front of the representation of Isis, the Great Mother: it is the Osirified Spirit, ATMU or SAHU. It is man with the possibility of recovering his lost stature of a God, of being Osiris-Ani, the God-Man. It is the Highest Mystery, the Spiritual Cause of Man himself. It is the part of Man which remains unchanged throughout his reincarnations and the different forms which Natural Magic obliges him to adopt in the course of his human and cosmic journey.

On the higher plane appear several Gods seated on their Perfect Cubes, with their attributes, all of them holding the WAS or staff enabling them to walk in the Invisible, which for humans in "darkness". This staff is an attribute related to Anubis and ends at the top with a simplified representation of his head; its base opens out in two parts which represent *the feet of the Goose,*

the feet which can walk over the mire, overcome the mud of chaos, *the Enemies, the Need for Food.*

In Thebes, as in all Egypt, these Seven Principles were also represented in the general characteristics of the Temples. And since the Temples were at the same time the mansions of the Gods and of the men who wished to become Gods again, the format is similar. The Temples fulfilled another function in their more external sections; they were places for the faithful to congregate in, and according to the festivals, the participation of the people varied.

We shall attempt to make it clear - or at least give our version gathered from ancient sources and without further interpretations that in Egypt, contrary to current belief, the Priests, whatever their degree and discounting the human failings which have always existed, exist and will exist until the end of time, were not father-oppressors of the people, but Fathers in the true sense of the word and in its spiritual aspect. The so-called "class struggle" is an intellectualized invention of the 18th-19th centuries and one which in the 20th has been converted into a dogma. "Classes" do not exist; what do exist are differences, like those which there are between a child, an elderly person, a man, a woman. And in some way, however imperfectly, due to the fact that we are human, there also exist Love and Religious feeling, and a Living Mysticism which brings all people together and through that unity gives them strength. For Egypt, the World was not motionless, but in movement, and every effort was made to ensure that that movement was forward and upward, providing everyone with a greater capability for perceiving his Self, and giving everyone the opportunity to participate to the fullest

Page 99 ▶
Reconstruction of a workshop dedicated to the manufacture of "ushabtis" and funerary statues

possible extent in this wonderful and tragicomical adventure which is life on Earth.

When a man knelt down before a Priest or pressed his forehead against the dust in front of a Pharaoh, he was not prostrating himself before them as men of power, but before what they represented... ultimately God, the Sacred Crown of those same people who knelt or lay in prostration. In all of this there were things that have almost been forgotten today: Devotion, Humility, Kindness, Love.

As among the Incas and among so many other peoples of the past, in "historical" Egypt everything that was produced was divided into three parts: one for the person who produced it, the other for the State-Pharaoh and a third for the State-priesthood. The first thing that strikes us as strange is that anyone could live from a third of what he produces... but in the years when this is being written no one should be surprised, since there are millions of people who live comfortably without producing anything. Moreover, it is unfair to attribute an imaginary poverty to the Egyptian people, since they enjoyed all the basic necessities, something which cannot be said today for around a thousand million people. But when years of drought arrived, or frontier wars prevented men from sowing or harvesting in time... then, as if by magic, enormous water containers were connected to the Nile, or the grain that had been stored in the *Granaries of Amon* was distributed. Thus, the former gift had become converted into a form of savings, except for the wealth employed in public works or in the upkeep of the machinery of State, another fact which should not cause excessive surprise to those of us who are living in the latter part of the

20th century. When we reaffirm that there were no slaves in Ancient Egypt, we wish to give a picture which is closer to reality than the more or less "cinematographic" fantasy which has become popular about the exploitation by an aloof minority who took advantage of the superstition and ignorance of a people who obeyed with gritted teeth and dreamt of claiming their social rights. We are sorry if these explanations go against the beliefs of some readers... but there naturally comes a time when children have to be told that they were not born under a gooseberry bush. Lies, though sometimes necessary, have like all things a limited span of life.

We cannot take any one Temple in particular to explain the symbolism of its parts, since the additions and repairs that those colossal works have undergone over the millenniums make them inappropriately confusing for the simple observation which we are now about to embark upon, so we shall take as our example a temple-type from Thebes, described in a simplified form which nevertheless conforms to the essential and original design.

The image of the Universe in this and other beliefs, the Temple likewise had seven parts.

1) The way leading to the Temple, which is an avenue lined sometimes with sphinxes and sometimes with solar rams or with simple monoliths. They represent *the Physical,* suggesting by their attitude which is the way that leads to the Temple properly speaking.

2) The Pylon or Pylons: they represent the porticoes which both join and separate the human world to and from the divine world. It is the approach to *the Sacred,*

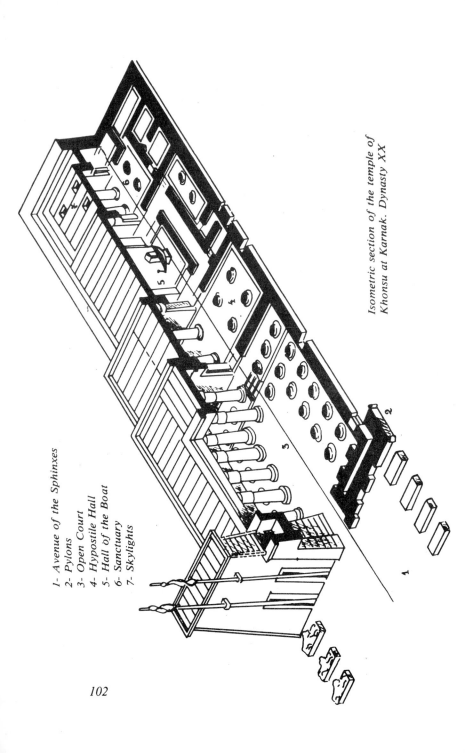

1- Avenue of the Sphinxes
2- Pylons
3- Open Court
4- Hypostile Hall
5- Hall of the Boat
6- Sanctuary
7- Skylights

Isometric section of the temple of
Khonsu at Karnak. Dynasty XX

with its great planes which vitally reflect the light of the Sun, and its streaming pennants fluttering high up on the poles attached to the outer walls, like tongues of the Word expressing life and unceasing movement.

Avenue of the Sphinxes, ending at the Pylon, at the entrance of the temple of Luxor. New Kingdom

3) The open-air court, surrounded by numerous columns carved and coloured with the different scenes of life with its emotions, its victories and its defeats.

4) The Hypostile Hall, generally small and secluded, where light and shadow play together, to express the double role of a bridge between the external 'and the internal. It is closed off at the end by a wall with a comparatively narrow door. Beyond lies the World of Mystery.

5) The Hall of the Boat, where in effect a ritual boat was kept, sometimes in a shrine of brightly polished

stones. It is the vehicle for the change of dimension, for now there is no more of the heavy and bulky grandeur of manifested life. Decorated with figures of Gods, it enables one to sail across the Starry Firmament on the *Blue Nile*. It was frequently veiled by semi-transparent curtains, and around it burned incense and different resins in the incense burners, to give the sensation of volatile waters impregnated with magic and mystery. However, in an underground part of the Temple another boat was kept, but this is not the time to speak of it.

Hall of the Boat. Processional litter in the form of a boat with the image of the God Horus at the prow. Temple of Edfu. Ptolemaic epoch

6) What we could call the Sanctuary, hidden away at the rear of the Temple, like an initiatic crypt bathed in Solar Light. It is the *Holy Place* where the Recondite Rites were performed. As a complement, at the back

and at the sides, it had chapels designed for different ceremonies, for the sacralization of consecrated objects and for the vows of service to God. It was from there that the Soul, in spite of being enclosed in a body, or rather chained to it, arose free and powerful, in the fullness of its conscious mortality.

7) The Openings in the roof, generally shaped like funnels, let the rays of the Sun shine through at fixed intervals, so that at different times of day determined by the way they were positioned, the sun would light up the images of different Gods or specific spots on the ground, performing the same purpose as, millenniums later, was fulfilled by the glass windows of the Gothic cathedrals, illuminating hidden signs on the floor.

This basic plan was complemented by different chapels and shrines. The Pharaoh and his dignitaries did not enter the Temple by the gate of the pylons, but from the left side of the Temple, directly into the Hall or court, to receive the devotion and affection of their people, immersed in reverent silence.

There were also rooms below ground, and a number of other shrines on the terraces at the rear of the Temple.

In general, when the Temple conformed to this typically Theban layout, the roofs tended to decrease in height along the length of the temple, in the likeness of the Primordial cavern. Apart from the High Priests who lived below ground, the Priests lived in buildings adjoining the Temple in cell-like rooms. Sacred Lakes, enchanted gardens and obelisks capped by ''sheaths'' of orichalc (electrum was the name given by the Greeks to this alloy which seems impossible to us today on account of its proportions between gold and silver, with

the addition of some ultra-heavy metal), followed by certain hieroglyphics which stood out slightly below the pyramidon, completed the picture.

The Temples, like people, lived in families. Thus, they were linked with one another by avenues, as in the case of the Temple of Karnak with that known as Luxor, or by "pathways" in the water of the Nile. There also existed underground passages, although hardly any of these have survived, since most of them were filled in by the last Priests, and the rest remained buried amidst the rubble or under sands and silt deposits of the ages.

Since the houses were single-storeyed or exceptionally with two floors, and had no major ornamental features on the outside, these architectural colossi would have been visible from a long way off, with their highly polished and brightly coloured stones, their pennants and their doors of precious woods and metals.

A geodesic interpretation is planned of the siting of the families of Egyptian Temples, as has already been done with those of the Mayas.

Another element to mention is the Libraries which were also housed in the Temples and their adjoining buildings. There, on stones, tablets and papyri, not only histories, but also meticulous records of all natural phenomena were kept. The very walls and roofs of the Temples tend to retain enormous quantities of astronomical, historical, theological and magical information.

The papyri are of a relatively late date. They were crafted from the triangular section of the stem of a plant; its fibres were selected, macerated and woven

together until they formed a kind of very strong and rough paper, perfectly suited for writing and drawing with a fine brush. Still today, in the outskirts of Cairo, anyone who asks can go and see how a papyrus is made, although the modern ones cannot compete with the ancient ones, some of which were treated with beeswax and very fine talcum powder.

Fragment of a papyrus

The most important papyri were kept, even in the times of the Library of Alexandria - as the first fire revealed - under covers of an incombustible material which might have been asbestos stone fibre. Cleopatra herself actually complained that her ancestors (she was in fact referring to the Egyptians and not to the Greeks) had not protected all the papyri with those coverings, since had this been the case, the fire would not have affected them... One more secret which Egypt took with

it since today we have no trace of or we are unable to recognize those formidable protective covers. Of the papyri, however, thousands of fragments have remained, though there are very few that are complete or that have not been reused in very late times for the everyday necessities of book-keeping and correspondence.

We think it is necessary to say, regarding the important ancient papyri which were kept in the Temples, that the ability to read them does not depend only on the various types of hieroglyphics (many of which are unreadable), but also on the colours in which they are painted. There also existed numerous codes based on the reading of groups of characters at fixed intervals or in reverse progression. Even on the simple scarab seals there are secret phrases and teachings over which the specialists torment themselves, generally in vain.

THE ESOTERIC PURPOSE
OF MUMMIFICATION AND
FUNERARY OFFERINGS

We have touched on this point very briefly before. We shall now do so more fully.

Mummification in Egypt is not a unique case in History; other ancient peoples have practised it, though with different techniques. Nor was it the same down the centuries in Egypt itself, and we would reiterate that at the beginning of what we could call the "historical era" it was only performed on the sacralized bodies of the Pharaohs or of the Great Priests.

We would also reaffirm that, for the Egyptians, death and life were no more than two sides of the same coin, even if the invention of this saying came much later. There is only one Life... which glides along on its two feet, life and death... repeating the cycle as long as there is a road to be travelled, finally to merge with the Soul of the World, the Solar Spirit, Amon-Ra, where

the King of the World dwells, on the Cosmic level: *Osiris-who-has-only-one-foot.* For the first mummification, according to tradition, was performed by Anubis himself - a prehistoric Deity - on the body of Osiris, who had been killed and torn to pieces by Set (differentiation), an operation in which he is aided by the Magician Isis, the Sister-Wife of Osiris. However, the sexual member of Osiris could not be found (this is the explanation of certain mutilations found on mummies), and it is Horus the Elder, the Great Bird of the Spirit, who finds it, and carrying it in his talons touches the shoulder of the Virgin Isis with his wing, causing her to become pregnant with horus the Younger. The phallus of Osiris disappeared in the Nile (it became identified with the River), Horus the Elder returned to his cosmic abode, and Isis endowed the newly born son (who like all sons of God is born of a Virgin) with Extraordinary Powers to unite Heaven and Earth, as the very meaning of Isis' name would imply: Step-Step, in other worlds, *Staircase.* Horus the Younger does battle with his father's murderer - who is at the same time the brother of Osiris - Set, and forces him back into the marshes where he hides in the form of Sebek,the Crocodile-God. Horus loses an eye in the combat but that eye acquires a life of its own and thenceforth becomes Uatjet, the Protecting Eye, with its eternal tear of compassion for the living.

This Mystery Rite would later be reproduced on the Earth.

The body of the Pharaoh, Prince, Princess, Priest or personage who had died, following the rites which assisted his or her Soul, sometimes by "putting it into" a statuette or jar (could it be this which gave rise to the tale of the Genie enclosed in a bottle, of Arabic

The God Anubis mummifying the reconstructed body of Osiris

Chest with the Canopic jars which conserved the viscera of the deceased

origin?), was subjected to a long and highly complex process which we need not describe here in detail. It was skilfully washed according to ritual and treated with antiseptics, both internal and external, which were introduced through all its orifices except the mouth, the eyes and the ears. The fleshy part of the nose was lifted off with consummate skill and the brain was drawn out little by little with a kind of hook. From the left side of the belly, the entrails were removed, including the heart and lungs. After many baths and treatments, the extracted remains, perfectly clean and immersed in aromatic essences, were put into four jars which the Greeks called *canopic*, their lids representing the four Sons of Horus (the Four Elements, the Four Forces): one with a jackal's head, Duamutef; another with a bird's head, Qebhsennuf; another with the head of an Ape of the Cinocephalus type, Hapi; and the last with a Human head, Amset. The latter, at the end of the New Kingdom, usually represented the deceased, like Piece No. 3610 of the Cairo Museum found in the tomb of Tutankhamon, whose face is probably modelled on that of Smenkhkare since many objects were accumulated in that tomb, for reasons we shall see, which had no direct connection with the buried Pharaoh.

These four jars were placed in a special chest which kept them upright and separate. The deceased, like Ra, was attended by five Genies, for enclosed in the jars and the one which was attached to the mummy in the coffin. The sixth Genie, related to Osiris, was the one who helped the "Double", the Ka, to escape from captivity through the false door in the tomb, which was sometimes activated by inscriptions; and in one case, personally verified, by highly magnetic fragments of an

aerolite. The seventh Genie was the most esoteric, was never named and had a specific mission in the Weighing of the Heart.

Mummiform sarcophagus. Inside each of the canopic jars was a little sarcophagus like this one which contained the viscera corresponding to the jar in question. Tomb of Tutankhamon. Dynasty XVIII. Cairo Museum.

The body thus prepared was very carefully bandaged with incredibly long strips of royal linen crossed over one another in ceremonial fashion. On them, and on the hoods and shrouds of ceramic fibre, magical phrases and amulets were placed in order to prevent the body from following the Soul. Its two legs were finally tied together as if they were one, adopting the Osirian posture. The skin of the soles of the feet was removed and replaced by sandals of papyrus and of royal linen, sometimes with eyes, so that it would not make a false step or ever walk upon the Earth again. The heart of flesh was replaced by one of ceramic, stone, or some other consecrated material, so that there would be some non-carnal symbol of resurrection. The arms were crossed in different positions depending on the degree and

sex of the deceased, and the time of year when the embalming had been carried out, this being, as the word indicates, merely an "act of placing in balms".

The fact that the deceased person bore on his body signs of resurrection and that weapons, furniture, food and drink were laid out beside him, has created the false image that the Egyptians were preparing the body so that, when the Final Day arrived, it could arise like a robot and enjoy the pleasures of mortal life. Such a conception would have horrified the Egyptians: the people because of their superstition, and the Priests because of their Wisdom. Only in a materialistic form of culture like the one in which we are living would people try to hibernate sick old people in the hope, once cures have been discovered for their diseases, of bringing them back to a life both ephemeral and completely disconnected from their natural environment. Nor did they entertain the belief of the Christians in a resurrection of the flesh, since their profound observation of Nature had taught them the law of cycles and the renewals or reincarnations of a single Soul, though through new, healthy and young carnal vehicles.

This ritual, carried out on the Earth, was intended to be reflected in the *Other Land* or Amenti. Their thought-forms had not stopped at building Temples and Roads in this World, but had continued into the other, as we can see from the *Maps of Amenti* reproduced on so many coffins and in their Sacred Books, where advice is given to enable the Soul to cross the portals of adversity in this and the other life.

As an example for this life, we shall take the formidable Negative Confession, a monument of a spiritual guide for any Aspirant to Self-Realization.

THE NEGATİVE CONFESSION: I (Nu Papyrus)

Homage to thee, O Great God, thou Lord of double
Maati (Truth and Justice).

I have come to thee, O my Lord, and I have brought
myself hither.

That I may behold thy beauties.

I know thee, and I know thy name and I know the
names of the two and forty gods (1)
who exist with thee in this Hall of double Maati;
who live as warders of sinners and who feed upon
their blood on the day when the lives of men are
taken into account in the presence of the god Un-
nefer (Osiris).

In truth "Rekhti-merti-neb-Maati" (i.e. twin sisters with
two eyes, ladies of double Maati) (2) is thy name.

In truth I have come to thee, and I have brought Maat
(i.e. right and truth) to thee, and I have destroyed
wickedness for thee...

[I have not done evil to] mankind.

I have not oppressed the members of my family,

I have not wrought evil in the place of right and truth.

I have had no knowledge of worthless men.

I have not wrought evil.

I have not made others perform excessive labours for
me.

I have not made to be the first consideration of each
day that excessive labour should be performed for
me.

---

1) The forty-two gods made up the Jury when a soul was judged
in the presence of Osiris. In another aspect they are "the 99 names"

2) Isis-Nephthys and in another key Nur-Nut (there are five more
keys).

I have not brought forward my name for exaltation to honours.

I have not ill-treated servants.

[I have not thought scorn of God.]

I have not defrauded the oppressed one of his property.

I have not done that which is an abomination unto the gods.

I have not caused harm to be done to the servant by his chief.

I have not caused pain.

I have made no man to suffer hunger.

I have made no one to weep.

I have done no murder. I have not given the order for murder to be done for me.

I have not inflicted pain upon mankind.

I have not derauded the temples of their oblations.

I have not purloined the cakes of the gods.

I have not carried off the cakes offered to the *Khus* (Sanctified Spirits).

I have not committed fornication.

I have not polluted myself in the holy places of the god of my city nor diminished from the bushel.

I have neither added to nor filched away land.

I have not encroached upon the fields [of others].

I have not added to the weights of the scales [to cheat the seller].

ı have not misread the pointer of the scales [to cheat the buyer].

I have not carried away the milk from the mouths of children.

I have not driven away the cattle which were upon their pastures.

I have not snared the feathered fowl of the preserves of the Gods.

I have not caught fish [with bait made of] fish of their
    kind.

I have not turned back the water at the time [when it
    should flow].

I have not cut a cutting in a canal of running water.

I have not extinguished a fire [or light] when it should
    burn.

I have not violated the times [of offering] the chosen
    meat offerings.

I have not driven off the cattle from the property of
    the gods.

I have not repulsed God in his manifestations.

I am pure. I am pure. I am pure. I am pure.

My purity is the purity of that great *Bennu* (Phoenix)
    which is in the city of Suten-henen (Heracleopolis),
    for, behold, I am the nose of the God of the winds,
    who maketh all mankind to live on the day when the
    Eye (Utchat) of Ra, is full in Annu (Heliopolis) at
    the end of the second month of the season Pert (i.e.
    the season of growing) [in the presence of the divine
    Lord of this Earth].

I have seen the Eye of Ra when it was full in Annu,
    therefore let not evil befall me in this land and in

*Fragment of a
papyrus. Scene
from the
Negative
Confession from
the "Book of the
Dead"*

this Hall of double Maati, because I, even I, know the Name[s] of these gods who are therein [and who are the followers of the great god] (of Truth and Justice).

And for the Soul, the following fragments from the same book commonly called that *Of the Dead,* which is combined with that *Of the Doors.*

THE COMING FORTH OF THE SOUL INTO THE LIGHT OF DAY

The doors of heaven are opened for me and the doors of earth are opened for me...

The bars and bolts of Seb (1) are opened for me, and the first temple hath been unfastened for me by the god Petra.

Behold, I was guarded and watched, [but now] I am released (2);

Behold, his hand had tied cords round me and his hand darted upon me in the earth.

Re-hent (the entrance to the Canals and Currents) hath been opened for me and Re-hent hath been unfastened before me.

Re-hent hath been given unto me, and I shall come forth by day into whatsoever place I please.

....

Behold, I have gained the mastery over my heart ("ib")

1) Seb, God of the Earth, plays an important role in the Otherworld watching over the first steps of the deceased

2) An allusion to the freedom and responsibility assumed by the Initiate.

I have gained the mastery over my breast ("hati"). (1)
I have gained the mastery over my two hands;
I have gained the mastery over my two feet;
I have gained the mastery over my mouth;
I have gained the mastery over my whole body;
I have gained the mastery over sepulchral offerings;
I have gained the mastery over the waters;
I have gained the mastery over the air;
I have gained the mastery over the canal;
I have gained the mastery over the river and over the land;
I have gained the mastery over the furrows;
I have gained the mastery over the male workers for me;
I have gained the mastery over the female workers for me in the underworld (2).
I have gained the mastery over all the things which were ordered to be done for me upon the Earth,
According to the entreaty which ye spake for me [saying], "Behold, let him live upon the bread of Seb".
That which is an abomination unto me, I shall not eat, nay, I shall live upon cakes made of white grain, (3) and my ale shall be [made] of the red grain of Hapi.
In a clean place shall I sit on the ground beneath the foliage of the ate palm of the Goddess Hathor, who

1) "Hati" is the *past*, the fixed Karma, the physical heart, subconscious and instinctive life. The *future* destiny, the realm of possibility, is "ib", the conscious heart, full of aspirations and desires, seat of the lucid will and moral conscience.

2) Figurines found in tombs in the shape of men, animals etc., known by the name of *ushapti* ("those who answer the calls"). By means of magic they were entrusted with all the tasks imposed on the deceased in the Otherworld, the Underworld.

3) The communion of the two species (solid and liquid) was expressed through the symbols of the colours corresponding to the Sun (red) and the Moon (white).

dwelleth in the spacious Disk as it advanceth to Annu (Heliopolis) (1) having the books of the divine words of the writings of the god Thoth (2).

I have gained the mastery over my heart ("ib");
I have gained the mastery over my heart's place ("hati");
I have gained the mastery over my mouth;
I have gained the mastery over my two hands;
I have gained the mastery over the waters;
I have gained the mastery over the canal;
I have gained the mastery over the river;
I have gained the mastery over the furrows;
I have gained the mastery over the men who work for me in the underworld.
I have gained the mastery over all the things which were ordered to be done for me upon the earth and in the underworld.
I shall lift myself up on my left side, and I shall place myself on my right side;
I shall lift myself up on my right side, and I shall place myself [on my left side].
I shall sit down, I shall stand up, and I shall place myself in [the path of] the wind like a guide who is well prepared"

1) Allusions to geographical places do not refer to the known terrestrial Egypt, but to their prototypes in the Otherworld, of which they are the reflections.

2) God of the creative and magical Word (Logos) and also of the written Word.

The highest hope of the Soul was, evidently, not to return to Earth for a very long time, although it was known that, except for Higher Beings, return was inexorable, since the Soul was not sufficiently perfected to become Pure Spiritual Light.

The offerings, of whatever kind they might be, were placed there for their physical use. As the Egyptians believed that all things had a *Double*, they were placed there so that their *Doubles* might accompany the Soul and serve it on the long Journey which, like the Subterranean, or rather, Occult Sun, it had to undertake in the darkness. This way why, in the funeral processions and during the psychopompic preparations, offerings were made to the Soul in the form of meals which, in their material part, were later eaten by the participants themselves, as in a *Communion*. Only what was kept in the inaccessible part of the tombs was never touched. But we know that in the funerary temples and in the complex tombs of the Valley of the Dead in the *Other Thebes*, the Priests of the Corporation of Anubis organized processions with offerings of flowers, perfumes, drinks, food and songs for the mummified Pharaohs, using the outer chambers as temples. Once the ceremony was over, the material objects which were considered to be "discharged" of their doubles were removed, then ritually destroyed and buried in nearby wells (modern archaeologicsts have found several of them); as regards the victuals, they were offered to those who had taken part in the procession and to the hardworking guardians of the Valley. In spite of the care taken to collect up all the "presents" for the Soul whose body lay at the end of the long funerary corridor, the early archaeologists found several small tokens, the most moving of these being little crowns of flowers similar

to those which are still used by Muslims in the sacred festivities of Ramadan.

As regards the litanies and spells which were used by the Priests in the Funerary Festivals, or the teachings they possessed about what happens to the Soul when it disincarnates, almost everything has been lost; whether by the deliberate concealment of what was considered sacred and secret, or by human folly, as in the case when the hot springs of Alexandria were actually heated up, causing millions of papyri to be set alight.

Something has come down to us, as we have seen, concerning the symbolical passage of the Sun-Soul through the Twelve Doors or hours of the night. This is reflected, to cite only the more easily accessible sources, in the so-called *Book of the Dead, Of the Hidden Dwelling* or *Of the Aduat,* with instructions for this and the other life, directions for the *hidden pathways* etcetera which had been known since the time of Thothmes I. The *Book of the Doors,* which gives instructions on how to pass through the Twelve Portals, is known from the times of Horemheb. There are others, too, like the *Book of the Litanies to the Sun,* where the Sun-God is invoked under seventy-five different names; and the *Book of the Opening of the Mouth* which describes magical operations on the statue and the body of a deceased person.

These Books, which are the main ones available at the time of writing, are only known from versions which come down from the New Kingdom and even later. We know nothing of other earlier versions, except from pieces of papyri which the specialists have generally not even begun to relate to *The Books.* At any rate, what is secret will remain secret, and it is as

Ceremony of opening the mouth. Book of the Dead by the scribe Hunefer. Dynasty XIX. British Museum

well to remember that the principal keys were never written down, but passed from the mouth of the Initiator to the ear of the Initiate. Or, at most, they were transmitted under cover of ephemeral series of geometrical figures of a Universal Language, some of whose forms were incorporated into the hieroglyphics of hieratic script.

THE OCCULT SIGNIFICANCE
OF THE SARCOPHAGI

The amateur enthusiast of Ancient Egypt tends to use the term *sarcophagus* indiscriminately where the specialists tend to differentiate.

In fact, this term has a Greek origin and means "flesh eater", whether because observation had demonstrated to that inquisitive race that a corpse, when placed in a coffin, tends to be reduced to bare bones in a few years, or because at that time people believed in the existence of a particular stone of Asian origin which had the peculiarity of consuming flesh, and in the case of coffins, human flesh.

Thus, when speaking of Egypt, we ought only to use the word *sarcophagus* to refer to the coffin which was usually in direct contact with the mummy. In the case of sumptuous burials, the latter lay perfectly encased within several coffins which fitted inside one another. This first coffin was usually made of wood,

and in some cases of thick board in later times. Only the outermost case was made of stone and unlike the others did not have a human form but tended to adopt that of a quadrangular box. In exceptional cases, of Pharaohs for example, the coffin would be encased within other larger ones, and the whole set finally enclosed within one or several casings.

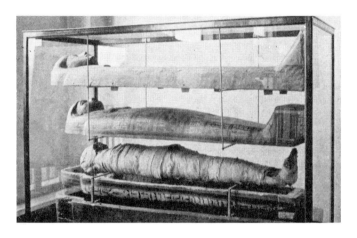

Double coffin of Usirmose, guardian of the temple. Musse du Cin-quantenaire, Brussels

In rarer cases, which unfortunately have not yet attracted the attention due to them from archaelogists, the coffin was made of metal, not necessarily gold as in the case of Tutankhamon, but also what the Greeks called *electrum*. One of these esoteric coffins has at last received a worthy and protected place in the Cairo Museum, having been inadvertently displayed for a long time alongside objects of lesser value. Its' shape is not exactly human, but a mysterious combination between

the sacramental aspects of the Horus Falcon and the human form. They would have been intended for High Priestes and were very specially prepared, so that they have to be handled with painstaking care, avoiding anything that might impair or jeopardize the Magical Form materialized in the alloy. No doubt to many readers this will sound like superstition and seem out of place in the work of an academic; but it is precisely we academics who know, leaving useless vanities aside, how little (often nothing at all) the Universities of the 20th century teach about these things. This should not cause us undue concern or diminish our optimism. It was the same with the Universities which did not teach that the Earth was round before the 15th century, nor that it moved round the Sun before the 17th century, nor that parapsychological phenomena were real before the 20th century. With the passing of time, many other things will be deemed good which are nowadays held in contempt or denied without sufficient foundation, simply because no room is allowed for any hypothesis which goes against prevailing beliefs.

If for the sake of simplicity we take the example of an anthropomorphic sarcophagus or coffin, we will see that it is normally covered on both the inside and the outside with hieroglypics and magical signs. Inside there are many representations of the Gods, especially of the Mother Nut, the Lady of the Starry Sky and of Light in the Darkness; her merciful wings - which relate her to the swallow-Soul - are positioned in such a way that when the coffin is closed, the mummy is enveloped in them. In other cases, like that of the famous alabaster sarcophagus transported to London by Belzoni, the figure of the Goddess appears on the floor of the coffin so that the mummy can rest upon Her.

The coffin or sarcophagus is like a ship for plying the psychic space which separates life from death. It is a protective casing against the winds of what modern "occultists" call the *Astral World*, avoiding contact with larvae and evil spirits. Let us understand that for the Egyptians, as for the esoterists of all ages, while the Soul is human it can not easily separate itself from the physical body or from the whole mass of sensations, memories and bouts of enthusiasm and unhappiness which earthly life may have engendered; it needs to be helped in its ascent in order to save it as much pain and effort as possible. That Occult Science was something in which the Priests of Thebes had become specialists.

There is nothing strange in an educated and intelligent person not understanding or believing in the necessity of the planes of the Aduat which were drawn on the floors of the coffins and sarcophagi. If in some unknown way it were possible to bring to the 20th century an educated and intelligent person from the Egypt to which we are referring and we were to show him the printed circuit of a transistor radio, he would not understand anything either; and if we were then to turn it on he would think we had music hidden behind some false door... In the same way, many "strange" phenomena which take place in the Museums in connection with mummies and statues are attributed today to sudden changes of temperature, mosquito bites, undiscovered poisons which had impregnated the objects or unspecified micro-organisms. We honestly believe that it is worth making an eclectic and unprejudiced effort, in this, as in so many other subjects, if by so doing we could increase our possibilities of gaining access to the truth, beyond the inevitable preconceptions which any age, whether it be ours or any other, contains.

Page 129
Sarcophagus with the Goddess Nut,
representing the celestial vault, painted on its floor

128

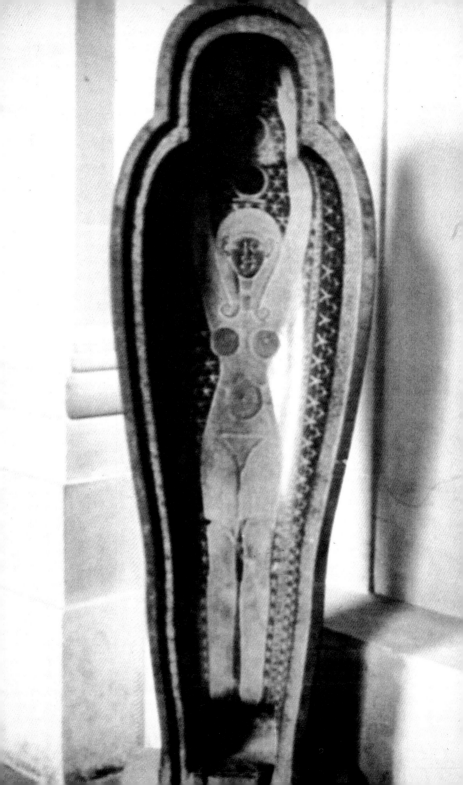

It is highly probable, to judge from isolated finds - including some in the clandestine antiquities market - that the ancient pharaohs, princes and priests, and in some cases high state officials, received funeral rites of an extreme complexity in the location of constructions which were remarkable for the beauty of their art or for the quality of the materials with which they were built. But the lootings which had already started occurring by midway into the New Kingdom, and the plundering which the tombs suffered at the hands of foreigners and desert bandits, have left us with only one example, albeit an extraordinary one, of the funerary splendours of those times. We are referring, needless to say, to the discovery by Carter (at the beginning of the twenties and financed by the unfortunate Lord Carnarvon) of the burial place of Tutankhamon.

This Pharaoh of the 18th Dynasty ruled for little more than ten years, after the disastrous experience of

Howard Carter and Lord Carnarvon demolishing the wall which blocked the way into Tutankhamon's funeral chamber

Akhenaten and his tyrannical order to worship not, as some of his defenders claim, a single God but one of the forms of the Sun-God, Aten, outlawing the time-honoured Mysteries which at that time were entrusted to the Initiates of Amon, at Thebes. Amonhotep (Amon-is-happy) IV, who on becoming possessed by his religious madness took the name of Akhenaten (Spirit-of-Aten), abandoned Thebes with his entire court for a city which he began to build at Tel-El-Amarna.

The truth is that Akhenaten did not reign alone, but had at his side a co-regent who has given rise to a historical enigma. His name was Smenkhkare, and so inseparable was he from the Pharaoh, that many are of the opinion that Nefertiti was no more than an official symbol. Today, now that the burial site of Smenkhkare has been discovered while Nefertiti's has not, there are scholars who go so far as to doubt that the Empress, whose bust, real or attributed, is famous for its stylized beauty, ever existed. Are we looking at a millennial version of what is today commonly called a "transvestite"? The only thing that is certain is that Smenkhkare's mummy was placed in a feminine posture and with feminine attributes, although anatomical studies confirm that we are dealing with the remains of a young man.

Whatever the truth about these intimate details, in times of great anomalies, the child Tutankhaten (the living image of Aten) succeeded his demented foster-father to the throne of the Double Crown, after the latter had either been poisoned or committed suicide by drinking poisoned wine. Under the tutelage of the reinstated Priests of Thebes, who had the support of the people, he changed his name for the one we know.

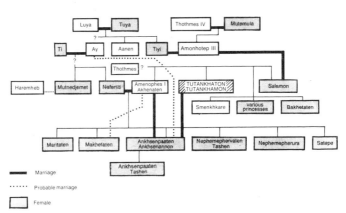

Luya	Tuya		Thothmes IV	Mutemuia			
	?						
Ti	Ay	Aanen	Tiyi	Amonhotep III			
	?						
	Thothmes	?					
Haremheb	Mutnedjemet	Neferiti	Amenophes I Akhenaten	TUTANKHATON TUTANKHAMON		Salamon	
				Smenkhkare	various princesses	Bakhetaten	
Maritaten	Makhetaten	Ankhsenpaaten Ankhsenannon		Nephemephervaten Tashen	Nephemepherura	Satepe	
		Ankhsenpaaten Tashen					

— Marriage

······ Probable marriage

☐ Female

Tutankhamon's family tree

He died in a sudden manner, for he had to be buried in a secondary tomb prepared for a State official called Ay (Eye), and it is debated as to whether he left any children. He was preceded, apparently for a very short time, by Ankhkheperure Smenkhkare, and succeeded equally fleetingly by the just mentioned Kheperpherure Ay. But we know nothing for certain until the advent of the military leader called Djeserepherura Haremheb, who was the one who set Egypt back in onder and made way for its last age of splendour, with the Ramessid dynasties.

Tukankhamon's tomb is small, so small in fact that its entrance became blocked up by flood deposits less than a century after its construction. Similarly we have no record of any remarkable deeds performed by the young Pharaoh; but it was through him that the Priests of Thebes endeavoured to restore their Spiritual Power in all its splendour, and at the same time lavished on

him a surfeit of protective charms in a veritable display of wealth and magical knowledge. The great store of objects of different epochs and natures demonstrates that this was no "normal" burial, and an enigmatic Destiny willed that it should come down to us practically intact; for the plunderers or the last of the revolutionary bands were only able to penetrate as far as the corridor and the first chamber. Perhaps the unexpected quantity of objects delayed them, and some patrol of the "Valley Police" surprised them, replacing things rapidly and calling a Priest of Anubis to come and place the Seals of the Jackal on the false walls which acted as doors.

It is to Carter, with the dubious funding of Lord Carnarvon (the latter was involved in, amongst other things, the illegal trading of antiquities: with smaller objects he liked to make jewels mounted in modern style before selling or keeping them), and also to the fact that the discovery was made at a good economic and psychological moment in time for the world, that we owe the good fortune of so many treasures having come to be exhibited in such an undamaged condition in the Museum of Cairo and later in many other countries.

This find gave rise to a strange dark legend, which there is no space to go into here in any detail, but which begins with the death of Lord Carnarvon in Cairo at the same time as his favourite dog in Great Britain; a legend which has still not been put a stop to, since the more or less subconscious terror which has been aroused by what has come to be known as *Tutankhamon's Treasure* has prevented many objects being correctly preserved. Even the mummy of the young Emperor is not, like the others that have been found, kept in the

Mummy Room of the Cairo Museum, but was removed to its original tomb, together with the outer sarcophagus which covers it and also the outer coffin which the tourist is only allowed to see by means of mirrors which are sometimes offered by some Arabian attendants... who never go inside. It is the only mummy known to lie in the Valley of the Dead at Thebes, surrounded by walls which had been painted rapidly but beautifully, in a style which still reflects some of the deviations of Amarna art.

Funeral chamber in the hypogeum of Tutankhamon

In the drawing shown above we can see how the coffins were fitted into one another and how these in turn were fitted into the casings. Carter and his skillful assistants had enormous difficulties in handling them

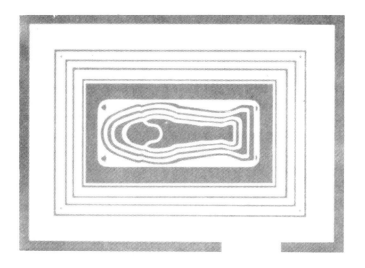

in such a confined space. But the craftsmen of Ancient Egypt had left valuable inscriptions and markings on the places where the coffins were fitted together... inexplicable if it had not been foreseen that the colossal *puzzle* was going to be dismantled and re-assembled.

Every piece of work carried out in this tomb is remarkable for its symbolism, its art, its craftsmanship and for the way it is finished, and moreover for the materials used, including a quantity of gold unsurpassed in any other known case. One might also mention that the Pharaoh's "favourite" dagger had a blade of meteoric iron... but that perhaps verges too closely on a magical bias which is bound to seem absurd to the modern observer (although the USA has presented many friendly Heads of State with a piece of lunar rock).

In our present work we can only show the cosmic harmony reflected by the sarcophagi or whatever we may call them in those cases where they cannot be classified by scholars on account of their untypical characteristics.

Although in the typical burials of other Pharaohs it was deemed necessary to place in the *Chamber of Resurrection* - which lay beyond several passages and crypts - the quantity of four casings and three coffins, or at least one sarcophagus, one coffin and the mummy properly speaking, Tutankhamon's burial arrangements were different. Partly on account of his having been, as we said, hurriedly interred in a very small tomb, and partly because of the singular politico-religious circumstances through which the Empire was passing, and which caused the priests to surround him with ritualistic complications, the purpose of which escapes us.

The containers of the mummy were positioned as follows:

1) An enormous wooden casing covered with stucco and beaten gold over magical symbols in relief.

2) Another similar one, which fitted inside the first. There is an allusion to the *Boat of Millions of Years,* that is the Sun which carries the Blessed.

3) Another similar one fitted inside the second.

4) This casing is noticeably smaller and plainer.

These four are normally kept in the Museum of Cairo. It is probable that they represent the Four Elements or Cosmic Dimensions.

5) Within the last casing was the beautiful sarcophagus of reddish quartzite, with its corners guarded by four winged Goddesses, fashioned in relief and related to the Four Guardians of the Corners and to the Eye of Horus, the Protector. It is the one which is in the tomb today, but its lid, originally made of Granite from Thebes, has been replaced by a thick sheet of protective glass. The original lid is also in the Museum of Cairo. A golden funerary bed was inside it, and it is difficult to understand how it was able to support the weight it had on top of it for so long.

6) In the first coffin properly speaking, made of wood overlaid with gold, we must pause to examine a singular feature: the Pharaoh's face appears, austerely represented, for the first time. It is still in the tomb at Thebes.

7) In the second coffin, also made of wood plated with gold, the face has a less rigid expression.

8) The first coffin, made of pure gold, has a weight in excess of 200 kg, the metal having been cast from a mould often more than 2 cm thick. It is encrusted with semi-precious stones, glass paste and small amounts of other metals. The face appears much softer and younger. It almost seems as if it belongs to a younger person. It has cunnigly concealed handles for moving it and lifting its lid.

9) The mummy was found in pieces in a very poor state of preservation, due to the effects of the ointments and resins which had practically reduced it to ashes, a fact which endorses the theory that the intention was not to preserve it, but to purify it.

Golden mask that covered Tuthankhamon,
mumy's head

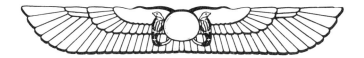

10) Another important object is the mask or hood of gold, made in a similar way, or perhaps to an even finer standard, than the golden coffin; it has its own characteristics and the face is smiling and is marked by its very youthful features. If we glance rapidly from the first coffin to the mask, we are given the impression that the Pharaoh is breaking into a smile and becoming rejuvenated, this cleverly achieved effect having a clear spiritual significance which coincides with the Egyptian beliefs that death offers the opportunity of ennobling the Soul and making it continually young.

The shattered mummy was bedecked with a great many ritual objects, amulets, gauntlets, rings, necklaces, statuettes representing the swallow-Soul...

Anubis at the entrance to the Treasure Chamber.

Veil-like pieces of cloth were found, like the white one covering the great image of Anubis on the Chest of Mystery. But there was hardly time to photograph them, because they disintegrated on contact with the moving air, although we do not know if this is true of all of them, since however incredible it may seem, there is no detailed inventory of the objects, apart from the list which was made by Carter himself and which has not even been properly studied. The veils which covered or were wrapped round some of the coffins were black when they were found, although pigments are known to change considerably. Apart from the linen, in its natural silky-white colour, all the other colours may possibly have changed.

We are not going to detail the great quantity of nails, handles, and plates of precious metals which were used to fit the coffins together. But we might point out that many of the *cartouches* where the name of Tutankhamon appears have clearly been touched up, which confirms the theory that many objects were re-used, and this applies to the tomb itself which is thought to have been rapidly enlarged to make room for the treasures. Although the burial of a Pharaoh could not be carried out until after the seven months, approximately, of the Sothic Cycle, it is quite feasible that the Priests of *Anubis lying on the Nine Enemies* did not exceed that minimum period. They did not, however, neglect to place the amulets and sacred metals, as well as the drawings *which-are-seen-in-the-darkness,* under the somewhat untypical paintings on the walls, as in all the crypts which have some connection with Traditional Wisdom.

It is remarkable how many model boats were found in the tomb, ranging from one which is no more than

an ingenious toy, probably belonging to the Pharaoh when he was a child, made in alabaster on a receptacle which when filled with water gives the impression that the little boat, powered by two dwarfs, is afloat, to others which pertain to Magical Ritual. Studies of their design reveal that there were some for sailing up the Nile, against the flow of the current, and others designed to drift downstream. Of course they were not referring to the physical river, but to the *Shining Double* which crossed the lands of Occult Egypt, of Amenti.

The other ritual object of iron - whether or not it was meteoric we do not know in this case - is a small

Alabaster boat mounted on a box representing an artificial lake.

head-rest placed in the corresponding position. Apart from these there were exotic and disconcerting things, like alabaster jars with figures carved inside them which are only visible if a lamp or candle is lit from within. These images of Man, who when his Spiritual Light is lit becomes transparent and his hidden powers, his inner Gods, show themselves, made the famous Osbert Lancaster say that the contents of the tomb reminded him of "the sale of the personal effects of a coquette of the Second Empire kept by a Jew with a taste for antiques"... which goes to show that Jesus was right when he advised against casting pearls before swine. But the present means of communication make this inevitable and the "specialists" are usually the most aberrant interpreters of a past which disconcerts them, and as vanity prevents them from recognizing their ignorance, they laugh at it in terms which sometimes stray wildly from objective truth.

Carter, an example of the contrary, that is to say, a good archaeologist and a good man, worked from 1922 to 1929 on removing all the objects with a team of restoration workers and specialists who packed everything they recorded and sent it to Cairo. The large coffins were transferred to the Egyptian capital in 1931. Carter, by then an old man, died in London in 1939.

With him the great archaeological epics in Egypt came to an end. The world changed, became poorer, more divided, and the economic capacity available to dedicate to the profound investigation of the past virtually dried up.

What are commonly called *Egyptian sarcophagi,* whatever they may really be, can be counted in their thousands and are now dispersed all over the world,

Page 143 ▶
Sarcophagi in one of the Egyptian rooms
of the Musee du Cinquantenaire in Brussels

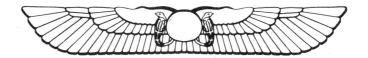

practically all of them coming from those old excavations of the 19th century and the first half of the 20th. Without knowing exactly why, people who love the past protect them and feel a strange fascination for them. In the great Museums, visitors walk almost on tiptoe in the rooms dedicated to Egypt and stop in front of the mysterious *boats,* absorbed, wonderfully ignorant, warmly human.

In their *Shining Doubles,* their former owners will have travelled for thousands of years in the *Astral Light,* and their purpose is now outlived. But they still attract us in this disenchanted moment of history, like a purely spiritual, beautiful, magical and ingenuous antithesis through which we can enter intuitively into the mystery of our own everlasting Inner Being, impregnated with Faith in God, in Nature, and in our own Destiny, where the origins and purpose of our fleeting passage through a particular moment in time and space is to be found.

An invisible Genius secretly whispers to us: "Man, be not afraid, Life continues".

THE HALLS OF THE WEST

We have described Thebes as bestriding the Nile, with a City of the Living on one side, and a Necropolis on the other. We do not know when the latter began as a real city, with its avenues, temples, guard barracks, ports, and so on.

Perhaps the West bank of the Nile has always been chosen as a place of burial, as this is in accord with the Sacred Books which hold it to be ruled by the *Genies of the West,* lesser forms of the prehistoric Anubis who was already in the Assembly of the great Primordial Gods when Thoth made man out of clay from the Sacred River on a potter's wheel, when the Souls of the Heavenly Bodies ruled over all and He guided the Forms of Light through the Primordial Darkness.

The oldest archaeological vestiges that have been found correspond to the 11th Dynasty, although it is in the New Kingdom and more exactly in its later period that the burials were to take place in complicated

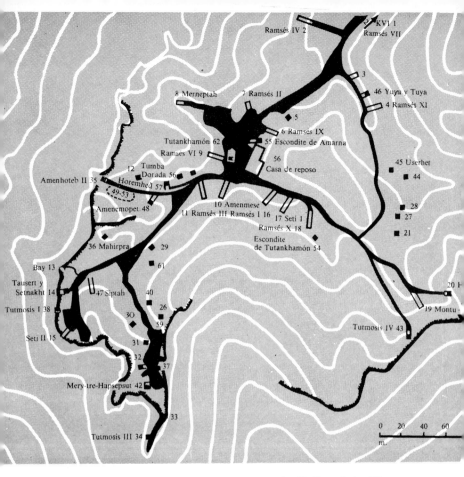

Map of he principal toms in the Valley of the Kings

funerary apartments. There were those built for the Kings, the Queens, and the so-called "Nobels", a generic and modern term which includes all sorts of people from Priests to outstanding craftsmen, singers, musicians, architects, soldiers, doctors, poets, and so on.

There are also thousands of tombs in the cliffs by the symbolic Western Mountain or Red Mountain, many of them almost inaccessible, of all kinds and of varying antiquity for all kinds of people, down to the most humble, including some belonging to the present-day boatmen and peasants. They are known only by the name of that vestige of the ancient corporations which is the little village of Deir-El-Medinet, although its present-day inhabitants are not descended from those of antiquity, being Bedouins who came to the place at some unknown date in the past. Nevertheless, these inhabitants of Grunah have a better knowledge than the professional archaeologists of the whereabouts of the old burial sites, and it is to their information that we owe practically all of the discoveries.

For them, the main source of financial income has been the sale of information about "Pharaonic" (as they call them) objects, and an unimaginable quantity of replicas, some of them perfect, like the three small plaques acquired by no less a person than Carter and which are today supposed to be fakes. The cunning of these people is, whether we like it or not, something to be admired. Some years ago a seam was discovered in the nearby alabaster quarries which had been worked in ancient times and then been abandoned, so that part of the material had acquired the beautiful patina which only the millenniums can give; these modern craftsmen took this alabaster and from it made some jars which

were so perfect that we began to doubt their authenticity only on seeing how many of them there were. We learnt of their contemporary origin afterwards.

Today more than four thousand tombs are known, from the ones formed by exploiting a natural fault in the terrain or a crack in the rock, to the complicated networks, covering hundreds of metres. The tombs reproduce in several ways the *Twelve Hours* of the Aduat and in general they slope downwards, following the text which begins thus:

"The writings of the Occult Chamber, the places where the Souls, the Gods, and the Spirits are. Those who do. The beginning of the Horn of the West, the door of the western horizon. This is the knowledge of the power of those who are in the hidden world. This is the knowledge of those who do: the knowledge of the Rites Sacred to Ra; knowledge of the mysterious forces; knowledge of what there is in the Hours, and also in their God; knowledge of what he says to Them; knowledge of the Doors and the Path which God travels; knowledge of the Powers and the annihilated ones."

This long path of Secret Teachings was represented pictorially in the great tombs. Similarly, the *Occult Place* or the Crypt of Initiation was represented by the place in which the sarcophagus was laid. The body was placed with its head facing West and its feet to the East, so that its *Shining Double* could hear more easily the whisperings of the Gods and, by raising its head, contemplate the Sun of Resurrection in Amenti, in its Victorious Dawn.

It has been confirmed that, just as the Books recommend for the crypts, the floors of the most holy places in the tombs were covered with fine, clean sand.

There is one detail which it is helpful to consider for the general interpretation of these portentous underground networks: and this is that instead of conforming strictly to a preconceived design, it has been shown that the architects would vary the direction of some passages and make changes of level in order to maintain a basis of solid rock. This is due both to functional reasons and also to the fact that the Egyptians understood the work of Man as being in harmony with that of Nature. Their respect, which we would to-day call *ecological,* was immense. For the same reason, though at enormous costs, the capitals in the largest Temples represent flowers which open out if they are in the centre of the construction, and flowers in bud, with their petals closed, if they are in a place far from the ceremonial centre of gravity.

*Bell-shaped column
in the Ramesseum*

149

The so often mentioned - and unfortunately so little understood and even criticized - *system of order* which the Egyptians had, was not an unnatural, inhuman machine, but quite the reverse. As they perceived the pyramidal order in the Cosmos and on the Earth, in Man and in all things, and the happy connection between causes and effects, which became in turn causes of other effects, they applied as far as possible the Numbers and Proportions which govern the universe to their own works, physical and metaphysical.

For them, the resurrection of the deceased in a world which was in another dimension, but was almost no different from this one, was not a hope or an act of faith, but a mathematical certainty. Of course, it is true that in the simple people of the villages and the countryside, faith replaces this Timeless Wisdom... But it was not farmers, shepherds or craftsmen who designed and forged the Egyptian Mysteries and gave out the plans for enacting them in this world. The people worked on the great public projects, as the people also worked on the Roman roads, on the Gothic cathedrals, on the railroads of the last century or on the aeroplanes of this. There always has to be an elite which takes direct responsibility for interpreting the laws of Nature and unequivocally directing how they should be given form in artificial works, that is to say, in works made by the art of men.

Nowadays a person steps into an aeroplane because he has faith that he is going to arrive wherever he has proposed to go... But the one who designed it, and even the pilot who is at the controls, not only have faith, but also knowledge and experience.

150

Thus, to see Ancient Egypt as a culture populated by fanatics and ignorant people who exploited one another, or to deduce from the length of the corridors in the tombs of the Valley how much influence the Priests had gained over the Pharaohs by the end of the Ramessid Epoch, as some scholars try to do, is pure "socio-fiction", something which never happened, except in a fantasy world distorted by the pressures of the present economic and materialistic preconceptions.

The great tombs of the Valley are divided, for the sake of simplicity, into three groups: of the Kings, of the Queens and of the Nobles, but all of them have the same basic design, developed to a greater or lesser degree. There are pictorial elements, like the Hecker frieze and the five-pointed stars in the sky, which remain standard features, and also architectural elements like the well, or a symbol of one, perpendicular to the main passage and some or many side chapels. In a number of major tombs, there is a wide recess to the left, of astronomical significance.

We should not give to much importance to Tutankhamon's tomb in itself, since in spite of its popularity it was not made just for a Pharaoh, and moreover it was rapidly enlarged, as we can see from the ceiling above the sarcophagus.

As has been said, the well is one of the permanent elements and therefore we have to see it as necessary and even indispensable. Was it in the physical sense, to stop robbers and the infrequent but dangerous possibility of water seeping through? Or metaphysically, as a representation of the Primordial Abyss and a device for attracting the telluric energies that come from the magnetic centre of the Planet?

Page 152 ▸
Nefertari's tomb. Note the decoration of five-pointed stars on the ceiling. Valley of the Queens

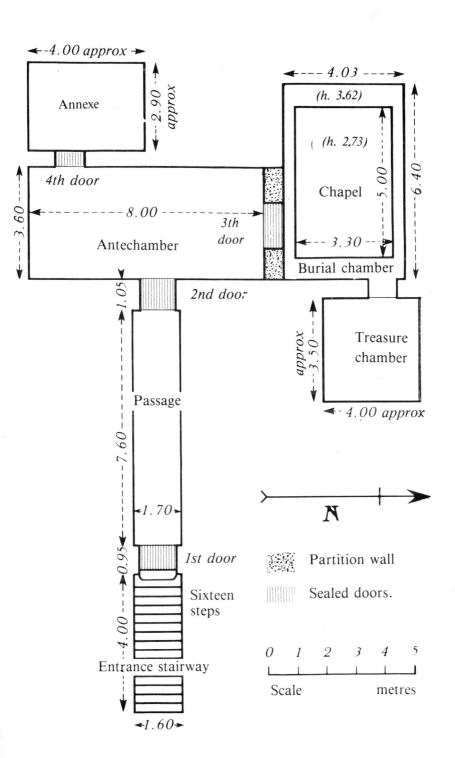

Annexe

4.00 approx

2.90 approx

4.03

(h. 3.62)

(h. 2.73)

Chapel

5.00

4th door

3.60

8.00

3th door

Antechamber

3.30

Burial chamber

6.40

1.05

2nd door

Treasure chamber

approx 3.50

Passage

4.00 approx

7.60

1.70

N

0.95

1st door

Partition wall

Sixteen steps

Sealed doors.

Entrance stairway

4.00

0   1   2   3   4   5

Scale   metres

1.60

If we situate ourselves in the canon of Egyptian thought, we will see that there is no contradiction between one thing and the other; both are complementary and it is most probable that both purposes were served by that deep and carefully built well. Regarding the concrete function of the wells, we know that they only half fulfilled it, since many looters, when Egypt collapsed and even before, by the light of torches and with the help of thick ropes, managed to cross them and get away with the treasures. The deadly traps and curses which according to modern newspaper serials and the cinema, the Egyptians used in abundance, are mere fantasies and speculations. Only at the end of its Cycle, or in times of political instability, did the architects have recourse to special devices to protect the sacred places. As regards the curses, they are simply non-existent; all that we do find, right back from prehistory down to the times of Cleopatra, are warnings, often symbolized simply in the Uraeus serpent, about the dangers of mocking or destroying sacred things. Translating this into modern terms, it would be the equivalent of the signs we put up to warn people that there is electricity in a place and that there is a risk of death for anyone outside the profession who tries to touch the wires.

It is, moreover, useful to remember an imaginary adventure which is sometimes attributed to Paracelsus, although the tale itself is much older, of Egyptian origin in fact. It is said that when the famous doctor-alchemist was in the city of Alexandria he saw the Plague enter with an empty sack over her shoulder. On questioning her she told him that she was coming to collect her annual tax of lives, which would be a thousand. The doctor-magician warned her that she must not take a single one more than Destiny had consented to her car-

◀ *Page 153*
Plan of Tutankhamon's tomb

rying off. The Plague accepted the deal, but a few months later left Alexandria taking no less than 20,000 with her. Paracelsus angrily confronted her with her deceit, and the Plague answered him that she had not broken the agreement, and had only taken a thousand dead by disease: the rest had died of fear... Could the same not have happened in connection with many mysterious deaths which are attributed to the "curse" of the Pharaohs?

The Processional Order which the Mysterious Books repeated in stone and paintings was affected by the fall of the New Kingdom, and the Priests had to remove those complicated magical mechanisms from their sacralized corpses, and then hide them away elsewhere, sometimes hastily throwing them together in concealed places. The Shining Double had already left through the "false door", and so the only thing left to do was to save the bodies from desecration by the hordes of bandits who had become impossible to control. Thus, in the 21st and 22nd Dynasties, for example, the mummies of several personages were hidden away: Seqenenra, Aahmes, Amonhotep I, Thothmes I, Thothmes II, Thothmes III, Seti I, Rameses II, Rameses III, some Priests of Amon and a number of others which remain unidentified.

In the tomb of Amonhotep II, the mummies of Amonhotep II himself, Thothmes IV, Amonhotep III, Meneptah, Siptah, Seti II, Rameses IV, Rameses V, Rameses VI and Queen Tyi have been found, together with those of two unidentified women and one child.

Small side chambers or chapels were also used to hide the treasures, as in the tomb of Amonhotep II, whe-

re the investigator Loret provided photographic evidence
of how some mummies had been thrown together, regardless of where they might fall, like that of a Prince,
which had crashed down on to an old Ritual Boat belonging to the original owner of the tomb. It is possible that we may never know the reason for these examples
of extreme haste and the persecutions and crimes which
must have preceded them. But what is important in the
context of this work is to demonstrate that the Priests
themselves, without prejudice to the respect they owed
to their ancient kings and knowing that they no longer
inhabited their mummified bodies, were only trying to
prevent them from falling into impious hands. This
contradicts the new-fangled materialistic concept which
tries to persuade us that the Egyptians thought that their
mummies were going to "resuscitate" physically. .

Only in such cases where it was possible, as in the
case of the mummy of Rameses II, the scribes would
make an inscription on the outer bandages so that at
some future date they might be identified, though stri-
pped of their wealth and even of their names enclosed
in *cartouches.*

Unfortunately, the looters found the mentioned hiding places before the archaeologists, who were only able
to salvage the mummies thanks to information from the
looters themselves. As a result, they are now in a piti-
ful state, despoiled of almost all their amulets and the
Scarab-Heart. This circumstance has also led to many
papyri being lost, except for the writings in *cursive,*
which were sold complete by the looters, instead of being torn, simply because they had no colour drawings.

Even on the restricted tourist circuit, one can still see the aesthetic and symbolic wonders of some of the tombs. One can still breathe there the mystery of those embodiments of the journey of the Sun-Soul through darkness and matter, terror and chaos.

EPILOGUE

In this little book, with its limitations imposed by our ignorance and by the age in which it has befallen us to live, we have tried to give the patient reader a series of disjointed views of that fabulous city which the Greeks called Thebes.

We have taken the opportunities offered by the subject to look for the true origins of Thebes and to make commentaries which have necessarily gone beyond the geographical sphere of that city to cover the whole of Egypt and even its possible Atlantean origin.

We have not written for the erudite; they know too much and have no need of these inadequate references; what they need is to clean away little by little all the mud of prejudice which has gathered around their knowledge. I have a fond memory of one of my old History professors whom, in my incautious youth, I once ventured to ask, in the light of the then new discoveries of fossils of fresh water animals and lavas which

had become condensed on contact with the air and which now lie thousands of metres beneath the surface of the Atlantic Ocean, whether he, personally, thought it possible that Atlantis had existed. After a few professional prevarications he confessed to me that he did, but that if such a hypothesis were to be officially formulated and if in addition one were to consider the possibility of its being inhabited by lost civilizations, many of the numerous books regarded as beacons of knowledge, would have to be burnt; and that his only ambition was to reach his retirement without any problems. Unfortunately for him, a heart attack prevented this a few days after our conversation, but I always admired his personal frankness and his truly scientific spirit, although the circumstances of his times made him conceal it.

The failure of so many social and political systems in this second half of the 20th century also makes it feasible to cast doubt on the workability of concepts which are held up as being infallible. Perhaps the only advantage of the collapse of the walls of this materialistic civilization is that, through the cracks, one can already begin to glimpse new horizons. With a healthy dose of humility we can begin to conceive new ideas which, as always, in this curved space and time, will meet up with their ancestors from the distant past.

From anguish arises hope, as from night comes day.

We are secure in our belief that many of the things that we have presented and which are bound to clash with established opinion, will find in many people the necessary echo to help them to reformulate the idea of ancient Egypt that they have received from their child-

hood upwards. For, as in every change of direction in History, time has moved more swiftly, and childhood has been left far behind. It is now time to face new possibilities.

For a long time now, I have been travelling to Egypt almost every year, not as a tourist or as a scientific academic researcher. I try to forget what I am now and to remember only that I am a philosopher, and that my Soul perhaps existed before the Pyramids were built and that it will continue to exist when all traces of these have vanished. Often surrounded by my young disciples to whom this book is dedicated, I simply wander across the old Land of Kem trying to see and to hear. Still today, in some places, time has stood still and the present inhabitants continue to reproduce the old customs almost exactly as before. When the oarsmen are rowing against the current, they still sing a few ancient words which have no translation in Arabic, and paint their houses and the oars of their boats in the same colours as thousands of years ago. From that peace, amidst the colossal remains of the "great shipwreck" of that mysterious Civilization, one can still understand certain things which are not taught in the books that are written nowadays and, what is more important, one can live them.

I believe in many things which my contemporaries es do not believe in and, on the other hand, they believe in many things in which I do not believe.

As simple as that.

They find pleasure in many things that give me no satisfaction and I enjoy many things which for them are worthless. I believe that we all have a natural right to be wrong or right about things. And, like Plato, I also believe that what is true for some, is not for others.

My academic colleagues know many things of which I am ignorant, and I know things which they do not want to know.

Some of those circumstances are reflected in this little book. It is my hope that some may wish to ascend to that philosophical state which we have called NEW ACROPOLIS.

My Soul bows down in reverence and drinks the waters of the Nile at the foot of the palm-trees, just as the Old Books advise. In the distance flocks of white ibis soar upwards and the Western Mountain becomes tinted with red as the fresh wind which formerly moved the Fans of Amon begins to blow. Perhaps not all is lost and we can, at some future time, live in a less polluted world, and once again lead a life of Spiritual Adventure. Thebes is not a physical place. Thebes is a *state of consciousness.*

BLESSED IS HE WHO LIVES, BLESSED HE WHO DIES IN THEBES!

BIBLIOGRAPHY

BELZONI, Giovanni. *Narrative of the Operations and Recent Discoveries within the Pyramids, Temples, Tombs and Excavations in Egypt and Nubia.*

BLAVATSKY, Helena Petrovna. *The Secret Doctrine.*

BRUCE, James, *Travels to Discover the Source of the Nile.*

CARTER, Howard and MACE, Arthur. *The Tomb of Tutankhamon.*

CARTER, Howard. *The Papers of Howard Carter at the Griffith Institute.*

CHAMPOLLION, Jean Francois. *Monuments of Egypt and Nubia.*

DENON, Vivant. *Travels in Upper and Lower Egypt.*

DIODORUS SICULUS. *Historical Library.*

FLINDERS PETRIE, Sir William. *The Royal Tombs of the First Dynasties. - Seventy Years in Archaeology.*

FRANKFORT, Henri. *Ancient Egyptian Religion. - The Cenotaph of Seti I at Abydos.*

GARDNER WILKINSON, Sir John. *The Manners and Customs of the Ancient Egyptians.*

HERODOTUS of HALICARNASSUS. *The Nine Books of History.*

MASPERO, Gaston. *Les Momies Royales de Deir-el-Bahari.*

MAYES, Stanley. *The Great Belzoni.*

SCHWARZ, Fernando. *Manual de Egipto.*

SPENGLER, Oswald. *The Decline of the West.*

STRABO. *Geography.*

WALLIS BUDGE, Sir E.A. *The Rosetta Stone in the British Museum. - The Mumy. - Baedecker's Egypt and the Sudan.*